The Essence of Research Methodology

Jan Jonker · Bartjan Pennink

The Essence of Research Methodology

A Concise Guide for Master and PhD Students
in Management Science

 Springer

Dr. Jan Jonker
Nijmegen School of Management (NSM)
Radboud University Nijmegen (RU)
PO BOX 9108
6500 HK Nijmegen
The Netherlands
janjonkermail@gmail.com
janjonker@wxs.nl

Dr. Bartjan W. Pennink
Faculty of Economics and Business
University of Groningen
Department of International Business
and Management
Landleven 5
9700AV Groningen
The Netherlands
b.j.w.pennink@rug.nl

ISBN: 978-3-540-71658-7   e-ISBN: 978-3-540-71659-4
DOI 10.1007/978-3-540-71659-4
Springer Heidelberg Dordrecht London New York

Library of Congress Control Number: 2010921307

Cover design: WMXDesign GmbH, Heidelberg, Germany

Printed on acid-free paper

Springer is part of Springer Science+Business Media (www.springer.com)

Preface

Methodology is the field which is indisputably complex. In the academic world, it is often said to be important, yet in everyday academic practice, it is not always treated accordingly. In teaching, methodology is often a mandatory course. Usually, it consists of learning how to adopt several common approaches when doing research, and how to conceive a *research design* (often leading to a survey). This usually leads to collecting data on a modest scale and – when the opportunity arises – analysing the data with the help of some statistics. Ask the students of their opinion at the end of such a course and they tend to heave a deep sigh of relief and say, "I have got through it." Then their real courses start again, in which methodology often does not play a role at all.

We are of the opinion that writing-off methodology in this way is a real pity. It ignores the valuable role that methodology should play in academic teaching as a whole. Here, methodology is presented as a form of *thinking and acting* that, while obviously entailing research work, can also include the design and change of organisations. This broad approach has been purposefully chosen, as it is almost obvious from research and graduation projects that the students do not really have a clue what methodology involves and, therefore, wasting their time by producing work that has a little quality. The successful Dutch edition of this book demonstrated the need to provide a brief yet concise introduction to the field of methodology. We sincerely hope that this revised and elaborated English edition can meet similar needs.

This book has not been written for fellow academic methodologists. It is mainly aimed at teachers and lecturers who want to pay attention to methodology in their courses. This may involve working on research assignments, explaining certain methodological aspects of specialised knowledge, as well as supervising Master's and, sometimes, PhD projects. Above all, this book is aimed at students who work in the field of management sciences and to those who are specifically involved in the studies that concern the functioning, structuring, diagnosing, or changing of organisations. The goal is to offer them a preliminary guide to define and carry out various forms of research. Our overall objective here is to provide the student with a clear understanding of methodology and its value for their academic work. Hopefully, it will also encourage specialised lecturers to actually assign methodology a more important place in their teaching.

As it is common in a preface, we express our thanks to all those persons, authors, and colleagues, who have contributed to this book. We are grateful for using their texts, ideas, and critical remarks. In particular, we are grateful to all (Master's and PhD) students who have had to struggle with various preliminary versions of the manuscript, as well as with the many ideas and notions "under construction."

Special acknowledgement is due to the former Nederlandse Organisatie voor Bedrijfskundig- en Economisch Onderzoek (NOBEM), a Dutch graduate network of universities that provided academic teaching to PhD students in particular with respect to research methodology. Over the years, this network offered us a systemic opportunity for cooperation in bringing a fine result in the Dutch edition of this book. We recognise the valuable support of Louwe Dijkema and Jacqueline Koppelman (both at that moment employed at Royal Van Gorcum Publishers in Assen – The Netherlands) who supported that first edition. This English edition is revised and rewritten on the basis of teaching experience gained since the first release of this book. We express our gratitude to Frau Dr. Martina Bihn at Springer Verlag for being so patient and supportive. We feel honoured to be guided by her.

We thank Anneliene Jonker who has spent countless hours working on the figures, references, and glossary. We are also indebted to Sarah Trenker who helped turn our original text into proper English. Special thanks also go to Jacques Igalens, professor at the IAE of the University of Toulouse 1 (France) who provided time, space, and company for editing the final version of this manuscript. Finally we acknowledge our academic employers. They have allowed us – admittedly sometimes under duress – to give courses outside the regular teaching schedule for more than a decade. Without this valuable support, little would have come of what initially started as an idea to make methodology more accessible to a broad group of students during their studies.

Jan Jonker and Bartjan Pennink

Doetinchem – Nijmegen – Toulouse – Groningen – Lasvaux – Appingedam – Tubbergen – January 2010

Please note: *Everywhere in the book where "he" is used, "she" can also be read. It goes without saying that this also applies for the term "researcher," which obviously includes both male and female researchers. The choice for the grammatical "male" form is not based on any form of discrimination whatsoever, but purely aimed on achieving a more readable text.*

Summary

This publication is designed to provide (Master's and PhD) students with a concise introduction to research, especially, in organisations. The aim is to familiarise them with the knowledge they need to make well-reasoned methodological choices when preparing an (applied) approach and provide them with the tools they need to develop what is referred to in this book as a *research design*. What methodology actually entails is explained by means of the *Research Pyramid*, which consists of the paradigms, methodologies, methods, and instruments used to collect, classify, and analyse data. Special attention is given to the process of constructing conceptual models. The guiding principle here is the distinction between open and closed questions. The notion of methodology is explored by looking at research methodology and intervention methodology. Both forms are examined in order to demonstrate the range of assumptions and choices underpinning a carefully crafted research design. This leads to the methodological *Box of Bricks* providing a schematic overview of the choices one can make while designing a research. Two interludes, respectively, between Chaps. 3 and 4 and Chaps. 5 and 6 provide some critique on assumptions regarding methodology in general and outline a multi-method approach.

The text as a whole is intended as an introduction to help students to understand what structuring research implies. The general assumption is that the students reading this text are engaged in organisation-oriented research – be it in a business or a not-for-profit organisation. It is structured around a number of succinct chapters and 15 figures. There is a summary provided at the end of each chapter. Each chapter also contains a compact overview of references to other textbooks and/or websites specialising in specific themes such as designing a questionnaire, applying grounded theory, or developing a conceptual model.

The book contains more then 50 practical examples, exercises, discussions, and short case studies. These are aimed at showing the student how to apply methodology in a specific context. Short footnotes draw attention to more fundamental theoretical, ontological, or epistemological issues. Criteria are listed that make it possible to judge the quality of the (research) results. At the end of the book, various checklists are provided to help students structure their research activities and reflect on key issues and choices to be made. A special feature of this book is an extensive glossary that provides the terms and notions used in this book.

This text is appropriate for courses on Research Methodology for Master and PhD students and can also be used as a part of the regular curriculum, e.g., Human Resource Management, Organisational Design or Change Management, International Management, Philosophy of Science. Extensive experience can be acquired by using it as a basic textbook for courses focusing on the preparation of a thesis or dissertation. It will also be helpful for people who want to refresh their knowledge about methods and techniques.

Suggested Reading

This is a textbook on the essence of research methodology. It was developed over a number of years while providing courses and workshops to PhD students, in particular. Many – if not all – of these students were engaged in a variety of research projects in the area of management sciences. What we have discovered during this long period is that many of these projects are almost by definition of a qualitative nature. A rather qualitative approach is also used for this text, which aims to offer a comprehensive grounding in what methodology is all about. Originally, we set out to write a slim and accessible text offering an overview of the key ideas and notions concerning methodology. The success of the Dutch edition has demonstrated that we might have succeeded in achieving this aim. This English edition should also be read as an introduction to the field. There are plenty of fine and sophisticated texts available as additional reading in this fascinating field. This text is just a means of offering students access to the subject; no more nor less.

If you are a novice in the field (e.g. a Master's or PhD student), take some time and try to read the text as a whole. You will no doubt encounter many terms (and subsequent definitions) that you might perceive to be grotesque if not outrageous. Whatever happens, do not worry: that is what an introduction to a new field is all about. Do not let yourself be fooled by the deliberately simple language we have chosen to use; it is already difficult enough to grasp the meaning of methodology without getting buried under the avalanche of words and terms that seem to come with it.

If you do not have much time but just want an overview of what methodology is all about please read at least Chaps. 1 and 2; we think that it is mandatory for any reader. Elaboration on conceptual models is provided in Chap. 3. We have introduced the idea of an Interlude (there are two) to help give our journey a specific if not personalised direction. Chapters 4 and 5 can be read separately depending on the nature of the research you have in mind; they provide a brief introduction to quantitative and qualitative research. Please do not skip the second Interlude since it will offer you a short introduction to a multi-method design. Two chapters deserve special attention. Chapter 6 provides an overview of the different criteria the various stakeholders engaged in your research project might use. It essentially shows that it is practically impossible to live up to all expectations. Do not feel frustrated; handling these different requirements in a proper and justifiable way is what good research is all about. Be clear and specific about what you are trying to achieve. Chapter 7 provides a more theoretical discussion on the relationship between methodology and acting. In doing so it establishes a broader perspective of the role of methodology in organisations. We are aware of the fact that this chapter does not treat methodology in the sense of doing research. Still we consider it essential that anyone doing research in organisations should be aware of the more fundamental issues with respect to methodology.

It might come in handy to know that there is a final Chap. 8 enabling you to assess your work using a number of checklists. There is also an extensive Glossary helping you to clarify terms and definitions you might already be using in your present work. We like to stress once more that this book was originally conceptualised with a qualitative approach in mind. The research practice of students shows time and again that most business-oriented projects adopt this approach. However, we certainly do not deny the value of a more quantitative approach – as is demonstrated in several chapters and in one of the Interludes. In the end, sound research, no matter what kind of research it is, starts with clear-cut thinking and (conceptual) sense making. It is only then that an answer to the underlying question can be sought.

Contents

xiv

Contents

List of Figures

List of Exercises

About the Authors

Dr. J. Jonker is an associate professor and research fellow at the Nijmegen School of Management of the Radboud University Nijmegen (Holland). His main research interest focuses on organisational change, corporate social responsibility (CSR) and business strategy. He is a visiting professor at the University of Nottingham (UK), the Business Schools of Nancy and Toulouse (France) and Barcelona (Spain). He has written many books and numerous articles. He combines his academic work with business consulting, thus staying in touch with different problems, discourses and realities.

Dr. B.J.W. Pennink is an assistant professor at the Faculty of Economics and Business of the University Groningen (Holland) where he mainly teaches courses in research methodology and International Management to undergraduates and graduates in different Masters programmes. He lectures at several universities in Indonesia (Jakarta, Bandung). In addition he was a visiting lecturer at the University of Ouagadougou in Burkina Faso between 1991 and 2005. Since 2006 he is project manager of collaboration project around Capacity Building of the IFM (Institute Finance Management) in Dar Es Salaam.

They both have been lecturers in Qualitative Methodology for the Dutch Organisation for Business Research (NOBEM) between 1989 and 2004. NOBEM was a fruitful network organisation between universities across The Netherlands providing methodology courses for PhD students in the field of business studies. This book is based on precious and pleasurable experience gained teaching together for more then a decade. A concise edition of this book appeared in Dutch under the title "De Kern van Methodologie" (2000 (first edititon) and 2004 (second edition)) published by Royal Van Gorcum Publishers (Assen).

Chapter 1
Looking at Research

Abstract This chapter outlines the structure and topics covered in this book. The central aim is to teach students how to design and conduct proper (applied) research. Research starts by identifying the research question. The questions addressed here, are linked to the 'reality' of organisations. This reality is problematic for two reasons – firstly, owing to the nature of organisations itself and secondly, the problems that arise as a result of the processes of organising. Problems in this area need to be broken down into a problem definition leading to a research goal and question. We assume that if you have a clear understanding of the problem, you implicitly also have the solution. Problems in organisations are by definition linked to various stakeholders. Two of them – the client and the researcher – often jointly work out what the problem is. The researcher often has to navigate between the requirements made by the organisation and those representing the community of science – the third important stakeholder. Dealing with the various requirements of these stakeholders creates tension for the researcher and he needs to reflect carefully before taking any action. Subsequently, handling the framed problem properly requires methodology. That is what this book is all about.

1.1 Introduction

Imagine the following situation: a company's manager calls up your institute and asks if there is a student available to conduct research into the way quality management systems can be better implemented. By making this telephone call the manager thinks he has found an efficient and maybe even effective solution to his problem and, at the same time, has done the institute – or rather the student – a favour by offering a trainee post. Maybe there is even some money involved! Perhaps he also hopes that the student – once he is carrying out the assignment in

J. Jonker and B. Pennink, *The Essence of Research Methodology*,
DOI 10.1007/978-3-540-71659-4_1, © Springer-Verlag Berlin Heidelberg 2010

the company – will be able to observe the company from a new perspective, detached from the problem for which he was hired. He may also secretly hope that the student may also provide some advice that could lead to more efficiency in other fields.

The student will no doubt start off wondering how to solve the manager's problem in a responsible manner and how best to structure the. Other considerations will include establishing a way to investigate the problem cleverly (taking into account how much money and time is available and the requirements the research needs to fulfil) and in what way the company will benefit from the results of the research. More importantly, he will need to base the method he chooses for the research on previous academic experience. He will be confronted with many kinds of questions from the manager that will need to be answered properly. Many will find this a difficult task as students still often consider doing research as being a kind of secondary activity and inferior to the main topics being taught in a specific programme. Understanding and applying methodology only becomes important when it is time to prepare the actual dissertation or thesis.

In fact, however research is very important when searching for clear-cut answers, since a graduation project or dissertation is based on demonstrating the ability to examine a fuzzy problem that occurs in the organisational reality. In order to contribute to a solution the research will need to consist of a combination of theory and (research) methodology that needs to be elaborated into an appropriate and well-reasoned research design fitting the problem at hand. Combining theory and (research) methodology and turning it into a research design is certainly not a standard job – it is always tailored to a specific problem. However, if the methodology is good and if the actual process of research is properly conducted a decent piece of research can be expected. Decent means resulting in research that is useful in organisational practice and meets academic standards.

This first chapter looks from a birds-eye perspective at the different stages of the process of a (applied) research project, starting from the point when a client, teacher or tutor, launches a graduation project and confronts the researcher or student with a question. It then looks at the complex process which unfolds in which the following questions all play a role at various times:

- What does observing (organisational) reality imply?
- What does creating problems – problematising – mean?
- Who is experiencing the problem in the organisation?
- What is the nature of the question? Is it open or closed?[1]

---

[1]Throughout the book you will find us using sets of terms that seem to be opposite. The most important of these are: (a) open and closed questions, (b) inductive and deductive research, (c) applied and fundamental research (d) a qualitative and quantitative approach and finally (d) conducting the research 'through your own eyes' or 'through the eyes of someone else'. Although it might invite the conclusion that those terms are always dichotomous, it is not the reality. Still we have chosen to use these terms as being opposite to each other, in order to demarcate assumptions and positions thus providing an overview of the possible choices in

- How should the research question and objectives be elaborated?
- What is the nature of the research is – more fundamental or more practice oriented?
- Which would be the most appropriate methodology?
- Which methods and techniques should be used for data collection?
- How should one's own role and position be defined in this research?

One can dream up more questions but this is quite sufficient for a start. Answering these will provide a step-wise introduction to the fascinating matter of methodology.[2] Our intention is to show that proper handling of the methodological issues at hand, results in a transparent process between question and answer. These questions will recur in various ways in the following chapters, where they will be examined in more detail.

1.2 Looking at Reality

A single perception of reality does not exist. There is no explicit 'condition' or 'situation' that everyone interprets as universal reality. This may come as no surprise. Reality is a moving target! Anyone who looks around sees houses, streets, or a passing cyclist. Anyone who is deep in thought, if only for a moment, sees people, events from the past or a kaleidoscope of (private) thoughts. Anyone who is engaged in a conversation with someone else sees the person talking while using language, making gestures, bringing to the fore thoughts and using metaphors and other linguistics to get the message across. Whoever definitely knows what is real in the description above (and everything mentioned above is completely true) may be the first to say what reality is. So, reality offers by definition an ontological[3] problem: we all know it exists, we operate in it everyday, yet, the moment we are asked to define it we find ourselves faced with a Pandora's box: people have

---

the process of designing and executing research. This deliberate use is one of the pedagogical features of this text.

[2]By the way: throughout this book you will find a number of these footnotes each time elaborating a more fundamental issue. The comparative Glossary at the back of the book can also be helpful when reflecting on these issues.

It should come as no surprise that the task of giving a certain precision to 'methodology' is not straightforward. The principal reason why this is not simple is that 'methodology', 'methods' and 'techniques' are terms often used in a mixed-up, interchangeable and 'vague' way. While not mutually exclusive, each term has a sufficiently specific meaning, which is why considerable care should be taken when using them to avoid terminological confusion.

[3]This is typically one of those terms you can find in the Glossary. We define it as "the study of the essence of phenomena and the nature of their existence".

different perceptions of 'reality', they give it different meanings depending on their situation or position.

This book looks at organisations.[4] Organisations should be observed as a special form of reality. They are visible on the one hand, because when you look at an organisation you will see buildings, chairs, computers and people who are occupied with a multitude of things. On the other hand, it is possible to argue at the same time that is impossible to 'see' an organisation. Even with the most common theoretical notions such as 'hierarchy', 'processes', 'structures' or 'value chain' you still cannot see anything. The activities of people or the products they make in organisations (also often unclear – think about 'policy', 'service' or 'health-care' for instance) are only partially 'visible'. So, what does one 'see' when looking at reality in organisations?

Organisations are (deliberately) made by people. They are constructs or 'artefacts' created with one or more specific purposes in mind. Therefore, one could say: together people decide to create a special kind of reality called 'organisations'. Yet, what do people do when they create this organisation? These are intriguing and fascinating questions to which there are many different appropriate answers. For instance, one can consider 'the' organisation as a purely 'mechanistic' construction which, for example, produces cars, light bulbs or diapers. Conversely, someone else may look at the processes of man-machine interaction, linguistic processes creating action or the collection of forms of cooperation and how they take place. And yet all the people involved may be looking at one and the same situation at the same time and in the same organisation! We are touching here on a scientific debate called the nature of reality or 'realism'. Two fundamental positions can be observed in this debate. Metaphysical realism considers reality to exist independently of what people think, while epistemological realism considers reality accessible to researchers through the frames of reference they apply to a specific situation.

---

[4]How one can look at organisations is a vast field of study in itself. Perspectives range from mechanical constructs to loosely coupled systems, from micro-communities to 'mental prisons' or from systems of cooperation to deliberate entities enabling the development of competencies leading to individual self-actualisation. It should be clear that this book will not address these different perspectives. It is simply based on the assumption that organisations are a 'reality'.

> **Box 1.1: Looking at Reality?[5]**
>
> "The world of direct perceptions consists of bits and pieces, scraps and ravels, the low rustling of the central heating, a disgusting taste in my mouth, the pain in my hip, the red colour of my typewriter, the tapping of typing, the pearl-grey glow of the sky, my glasses resting on my nose, rain dripping down through the ceiling in the other room, birds in the sky, the sound of tyres of cars outside on the street, the titles in my bookshelves, this and that, now and then, a puzzlement of perceptions."
> *Taken from: "The Fourth Dimension", R. Rudy (1991)*
> Question: Are you able to define the position this author is taking in the reality debate?
>
> Organisations are the object of study for people such as management scientists, organisational sociologists, linguists and communication scientists. All these people look at and observe different aspects, issues, phenomena, parts and functions of an organisation. Moreover, they can all 'prove' that they can see the aspect they are studying. Perhaps that is why organisations are such an intriguing object of study. Nevertheless, over the past 100 years and more, many books (one can easily say complete libraries) have been written about what organisations are supposed and not supposed to be. The fact remains that we live in a society dominated by organisations – a society where the 'fabric' is constructed on the basis of organisations. Everything we do, buy, use, touch, make, sell, buy, utilize, throw away, burn, recycle or demolish is directly connected to the phenomenon of (an) organisation. Whether this is good or bad is not an issue here.[6] This publication departs from the (possibly simplistic) fact that organisations do exist – that they are omnipresent in our contemporary society – and, therefore, specific issues can become the object of a research. For us research starts by defining a problem even if this problem might not be what the research is all about in the end.

1.3 Problematising

A 'problem' – or a situation that is alleged as being problematic – in an organisation needs to be perceived first, before it actually can be referred to as a problem. It is spotted as a problem (in a subjective way) if someone is bothered by something: a

---

[5]Here you find another pedagogical feature of this book. We have added a bit more then fifty of these 'boxes' with questions, exercises, short checklists and more, all intended to help you put serious consideration into you own research design.

[6]In the past decade a vivid organisational and societal debate has (re)occurred on the subject of this 'neutral' or 'instrumental' perspective. The debate can be traced under headings such as Corporate Social Responsibility (CSR) or Corporate Citizenship (CC). These debates question the role, position and function of organisations in contemporary society. While management sciences address in general the construction (design) and effective operation of an organisation, these debates raise the issues of the wider societal impact of organisations.

situation, a result or specific behaviour. The person involved will say: "I have a problem", or "... things have not been running smoothly lately", or "If it goes on like this we will lose market share and then we will have a problem". If a manager then says he has an organisational change problem, then he indicates, and at the same time frames, an issue[7] that apparently needs to be solved. He (and maybe others involved) interpret this issue as something that has to change in order for the problem to be solved. Discussing this issue as a change problem implies an interpretation of the nature of that problem and a possible solution. If you have 'the problem' you implicitly have the solution! It is always people that have – or create – a problem. This suggests that a problem is always 'created' by people through their interpretation of a reality they are operating in. This phenomenon (how things appear to people and how people experience the world) is called *problematising*.

Problematising[8] is the process in which people in an organisation interpret a situation in such a way that it can be referred to as 'a problem'. It implies going below the surface of what has been offered as 'the problem' and trying to define what is really the matter. In the process of problematising they can make use of facts, figures, concepts, paradigms, opinions, experiences, emotions and many, many other things. Problematising therefore is not solely a rational process based on 'facts' but a lively mixture of what people have in their minds and hearts and leads to a biased and fragmented interpretation of the world. A process that implies giving priority to one particular problem above another; people involved have to make choices between more and less important problems. The process of problematising results in assigning a recognisable label[9] thus creating the problem as defined by a person or a group of people in the organisation. Problems are the product of people and organisations (random problems out in the open do not exist). It is the people in a particular situation that will call a specific issue, situation or phenomenon problematic. So a problem is by definition man-made. The result of this often very implicit process will be 'a problem indication' or 'problem description'.[10]

Organisations are constantly confronted with a certain number of problems with different degrees of importance. Some will simply become obsolete over time, some will disappear and some are selected for further inspection. But whatever is

---

[7]Framing an issue implies by definition the use of 'theory' of any kind; we cannot 'see' reality without bringing theory to it. A theory is a series of logical and related arguments specifying relationships among a chosen set of constructs or variables based upon or leading to concepts regarding a specific issue or situation (adopted from: Doty and Glick, 1994).

[8]The word 'problematising' is not common in everyday language. Still this process in which people perceive, elaborate, interpret, frame and label a situation in such a way that it is called 'a problem' is what problematising is all about. In brief, problematising is the process in which people 'make' a problem.

[9]This is called the process of reification: regarding things that are not real as real.

[10]Given the problematic nature of problems it might be handy to structure them in (a) the initial problem, (b) underlying problems and (c) fundamental – or hidden – problems.

done to solve them, problems will always occur. Organisations and problems are like cats and fleas. Some problems are tolerable ("In our organisation the coffee has always been awful"), while other problems are not and people feel they should be solved. Therefore, having a problem is not only determined by the 'concreteness' or 'realness' of the situation ("This is serious"), but by the necessity to have it put on the organisation's 'agenda' first. Problems, however specific and realistic they are, determined within a framework of 'politics and power'. They are based on the subjective and subject-bound interpretation of a certain situation. The idea that it is a matter of one clearly defined problem that all people involved agree on is an illusion. It is a poor consolation to know that all people involved with the problem (including the researcher) subsequently act on the basis of their own interpretation of 'the' problem as they perceive and interpret it. What is indicated to be a problem in the organisation therefore depends on people. By calling something a problem there is also a suggestion that the problem once defined, remains the same. Yet, just by referring to a situation as a problem, thus placing emphasis on a particular situation or group of people, may make the situation change. The mere act of selecting a situation as being problematic is an intervention. So, problems change during 'handling'. This dynamism is a difficulty that should be taken into account when trying to study and solve them.

Box 1.2: Who is Having a Problem?
Stop reading for a moment and try to provide a brief answer to the following questions (which assume you are already doing research):

(a) What problem (problems) is your 'client' actually confronted with? Make a short list.
(b) Which problems do you have at this moment (looking at this research project)? Also make a short list.
(c) Now make a brief comparison. Are you and your 'client' talking about the same problem? Are you certain of that? Did you check?

1.4 Problem Stakeholders

Problems in organisations are always connected to people. Conceptualising the different roles of these people in relation to the problem results in the identification of the following stakeholders and their roles: problem creators, -sponsors, -owners, -solvers and -subjects.

- *Problem creators* are people in the organisation who are able (i.e. have the authority and power) to put the problem on the organisational agenda. They focus attention on a problem and often attach a certain priority – a certain weight – to it. Once it is put on the agenda their task is basically fulfilled and they need to pass it on to others.

- *Problem sponsors* are generally people without a direct 'problem', but who provide a certain 'service' in putting and keeping the problem on the organisational agenda. Without their support the problem might disappear. Sponsors back up the problem notion (on the basis of various motives which may be political, financial or emotional), but in fact do not contribute to reaching a solution.
- *Problem owners* are people who are assigned 'rights of ownership' of a problem, voluntarily or involuntarily. An owner is appointed during the process of making the problem an item on the agenda. After the labelling has been established the problem can be passed on to the (functional) manager who best fits the bill. ("I see we have a staffing problem" or "I think we can clearly see a logistic problem here."). A particular phenomenon is worth noticing here. It can be really appealing to 'collect' problems; they provide the collector with a ticket to budget, power and 'status' and might even distract others from his individual shortcomings.
- *Problem solvers* are people who deal specifically with the problem: they are responsible for examining, advising and eventually solving the problem. Problem solvers sometimes have the (dual) role of problem owners, but most of the time other people are appointed as (internal or external) advisors, trainers or researchers. This classification is not completely infallible, of course, as examining a problem does not always imply solving it.
- Finally, *those involved* (or the problem subjects) – or the problem originators – are the ones the problem is about. They are the 'cause' of the problem. Where does the problem come from, whom or what causes it? The problem might sometimes be individual (a manager who has put his hand in the till), but most of the times it concerns a certain well-defined group of people in the organisation (e.g. a particular department, the sales force, back office people, internal consultants) who are battling with the problem. Curiously enough they are not always involved in the process of problematising. Those involved in creating the problem have a tendency to overlook the subjects; they talk about them but not *with* them.

Who has what kind of problem and when? What does the problem actually entail? Why is it considered to be a problem and why does it need to be solved? These are all questions that are generally difficult to answer at the start of research. They tend to be 'slippery' thus difficult to grasp. Given the fact that the actors involved will interpret the problem in (fundamentally) different ways, it is not an easy task to get to grips with what is at stake for which stakeholder and what the nature of the problem as they perceive it.

One thing is clear though: once the 'phase' of problematising has been completed, the result is a 'product' that has a name and label, and it becomes a transferable phenomenon that can be shared by different groups of people in the organisation. This definition takes place by applying a recognisable label, which is most often taken from an established body of knowledge within the management sciences (e.g. logistics, human resources, communication, etc.) and recognisable for the organisation. A problem should therefore be defined as the interpretation of a (empirically[11]) 'labelled' situation, condition, phenomenon or function of an organisation that is experienced as so problematic by those involved (stakeholders) that it requires (some) research to reach a (possible) solution. Maybe we could say that problems that do not have a potential solution are not problematised.

Given the nature of the process of problematising it is important to put the term 'problem' temporarily between brackets at the start of research. It is rarely clear what is going on exactly. Is it really important to establish, for example, who is involved, what the problem's consequences are, the possible effect or impact of a solution and so forth and how the discrepancy between the 'current status' and 'desired status' is interpreted. Last but not least, it is important to reflect on the 'ambition' of a problem. Do we talk about something that can be solved without much effect on the going concern, or is it something that is fundamental to the its operation? When the actual research starts, the only established fact is that there is something going on that has resulted in a (still ongoing) problematising process and subsequent problem formulation. Yet, at some point, the people involved in the problem have decided that it needs to be dealt with and that outsourcing, researching or contracting to others (e.g. consulting or training) is an obvious next step. Subsequently, people start making telephone calls, arranging appointments or sending e-mails. They move into action to handle the problem. It is then that the problem, as it is now defined, is discussed for the first time. We consider that the moment when the actual research starts.

1.5 Conducting Research

Conducting research entails the deliberate and methodical search for (new) knowledge and insights in the form of answers to questions that have been formulated in advance. Conducting research is a specific form of goal-oriented acting.[12] It is common to divide research into scientific and applied research.

Scientific research (or fundamental research) involves conducting research that contributes to general knowledge, knowledge that is expressed in the form of statements, models, concepts and (grand) theories. After defining the problem, the scientific researcher starts by determining which knowledge is present in a certain field (e.g. in the form of already available theory expressed in recognised

---

[11]Please observe that we have squeezed in the word 'empirical' here. Empiricism refers to a line of thinking where 'study of reality ... suggests that knowledge is gained through experience and the senses.' (see Glossary). It assumes that there is an objective and a subjective reality or one derived from 'theory' and one from practice.

[12]We will later devote an entire chapter to the relationships between organising, methodology and acting. The notion of 'acting' is at least as old as Aristotle. He states: 'the origin of action – its efficient, not its final cause – is choice and that choice is desire and reasoning with a view to an end' (Nicomachean Ethics, 1139a, 31–2).

publications), establishes certain shortcomings in the comparison between the question asked and the knowledge available, tries to eliminate these shortcomings by generating new knowledge and insights on the basis of research and finally adds the results of his efforts to the existing body of knowledge (e.g. in the form of an article or report). The fundamental endeavour in the generation of scientific knowledge is that it produces knowledge of a generally applicable (generalisable) form and that it is 'true' (valid, reliable, etc.).

Applied research (also called practical or management research) is research that engenders data, insights, methods, concepts and views – often derived from the knowledge gathered during the course of fundamental research – which are applicable for a specific organisational or managerial problem. Applied research strives (a) to obtain knowledge about a particular issue, etc. in the organisation and (b) to contribute to the improvement of that issue, etc. leading to problem solving.

The role of the researcher is to examine the problem as it occurs and formulate relevant (research) questions. Subsequently, he will search for various forms of support (in the form of theory, methodology and practical guidance), attempting to develop answers by means of these resources. Finally, he will then offer these solutions to stakeholders and possibly other relevant parties. However, this does not imply that the researcher who conducts applied research 'just messes around'. Applying specific methodologies derived from a more scientific background to practical situations is in itself also a part of science. That is called 'the world of design' (van Aken, 2004). Applied research uses the same 'methods' as scientific research. This means that applied research has similarities to fundamental research in the sense that it is always a matter of sound and justifiable work.

This publication revolves around the design and implementation of correctly executed applied research.[13] Research, by definition, starts with a question regarding a problematic organisational situation. Does this imply that once engaged in applied research one cannot switch to fundamental research and vice-versa? Given the fact that both kinds of research are based on the same methodological body of knowledge using identical methods and techniques the answer is still by definition 'no'. However a series of applied research projects can turn into truly scientific research while fundamental research can deliver outcomes applicable in various situations. It all depends on what the researcher has in mind at the start of his project, the scope, depth and theoretical elaboration of the researched phenomenon at hand. Whatever the case, any research project will start with a question. It is the nature of this question that guides the research process.

---

[13]It is common to make a distinction between fundamental and applied research. Research can be considered fundamental when claims about a particular phenomenon are valid and reliable for all situations and/or cases. While making use of the same methodologies, methods etc. applied research only provides insight to a particular phenomenon in a specific case. In itself this insight can be valid and reliable but can't be used to predict how the same phenomenon might occur in other situations.

1.6   The Nature of a Research Question

The previous section has possibly created the impression that the manager (or others involved), who detected the problem, has (or have) a well-defined and clear-cut 'storyboard' for the researcher to work on. In most cases, this is an illusion. Although the process of problematising may have engendered a 'problem', the problem will probably not have a clear form. The organisation presents a problematic situation that can be approached from different angles. Whose problem is it? Why has it occurred at this particular moment? How can you study the problem? Which 'theoretical' elements are distinguishable in the problem? Is it actually clear what the problem is? And to whom is it clear? These are the kind of questions that a researcher needs to ask when he accepts a research assignment.[14] Please remember: at first sight the problem does not need to consist of a well-defined question that is researchable. It all depends on the nature of the question. We find it helpful to divide between 'open' and 'closed' questions.

1.6.1   Open and Closed Questions

An open question takes a broad look at a problem, thus leaving ample space for various definitions. In the case of an open question, it is often unclear in advance what actually needs to be examined. The researcher's 'basic attitude' (see Chapter 2) in dealing with this kind of question is dominated by 'theory development' and 'searching for a grounded theory'. Moreover, the initial question probably might and will change in the course of research if not straight away from the start. In designing and carrying out the research, the researcher will strive to obtain a balanced understanding of the organisational reality to ensure that those involved with the problem in the organisation (the actors in the field) are assessed correctly. The 'theory' that has been sought and found also needs to be understood by the people involved and be useful to them. It is essential to realise when confronted with an open question that 'the course of research' cannot be strictly determined in advance. An essential part of conducting research based on an open question is mainly the actual clarification, but it is also about exploring which does not always lead to clarification of the question. It is only after a certain time that it becomes clear what the meaning of the initially formulated open question is and if and how it subsequently needs to be answered. So, the result of a research project based on an open question might result in a clear and well-defined question leading to the subsequent research.

---

[14]Implicitly we make a distinction here about someone enrolled in a regular programme doing research and a (business) consultant. Researchers just starting with research are not considered to be consultants. In the course of the project they might begin to act as a consultant, but that is all in the process of learning. Consultants are hired to solve a problem.

Box 1.3: Example of an 'Open' Question
What kind of 'mental images' do change managers' use?
How do they use these images?
A closed question on the other hand, contains a clear outline which needs to be understood and is therefore suitable for further delineation, for example, in the form of operationalising and testing hypotheses. On the basis of a closed problem the researcher will formulate one or more suitable research questions. It is these research questions that will be answered by conducting the actual research. They will consist of several conclusions that will be used to draw up recommendations and that may contribute to the solution of the perceived problem.

Box 1.4: Example of a 'Closed' Question
To what degree are people in the organisation stimulated by various incentives for motivation?

The researcher who conducts research by means of a 'closed' question (generally) operates according to a clear action plan in which the most important research activities are established in advance. You can think of the position – and use – of theory, the development of conceptual models, the operationalising of variables, formulating hypothesis, means of analysing data and so forth. The greater the emphasis given to testing hypotheses, the more influence the action plan will have on the actual course of the research process.

Using an 'open' or 'closed' question is neither right nor wrong. A question being open or closed depends on the nature of the issue being studied, it depends on the interpretation by the researcher and a variety of other factors. Yet, the nature of the question that the researcher poses (or is given) at the beginning will be essential for determining the subsequent way of working. An 'open' question cannot be tested; it provides a generic direction. A 'closed' question complicates (or even prevents) the involvement of the employees in the research. In the case of an 'open' question the researcher will make a sincere attempt to really come to understand what is going on from the perspective of those involved. With a 'closed' question the researcher will make an attempt to establish to what degree there only appears to be a problem (leading to counting 'facts' resulting for example in percentages). No matter what the nature of the question is, this triggers the methodological approach to the research. Working with an 'open' or 'closed' question demands a different basic attitude on the part of the researcher – an attitude that requires its own methodology.

1.7   Linking the Research Question, Problem and Goal

So far, the consideration of the issue raised by the organisation (and the researcher involved) is seen to result in many extra questions and a fundamental distinction between open and closed questions. If the researcher wants to progress, he should use this information as the starting point of the problem-formulating process. This process will result in a definition of the research problem, the research objective, the research question and the identification of possible pre-conditions. There are innumerable articles and books that examine the role, place and meaning of problem- and goal definitions as well as what a decent research question should comprise. Therefore, several (albeit limited) references have been included in the references that are enclosed with this chapter. The checklist below emerges sooner or later for almost every type of research and is often followed by an in-depth analysis resulting in more detailed questions. Here we will only focus on the issue of defining the problem at the start of a research project.

> **Box 1.5: Brief Checklist at the Start of a Research**
> Give a short description of:
>
> 1. The situation in which the problem occurs (context)
> 2. Your problem definition (at present)
> 3. The research question and which elements of the problem you are going to examine
> 4. Your research objective and what you are aiming for with your research
> 5. Any important pre-conditions that need to be met (such as e.g. time, money, and access)

1.7.1   Problem Definition

The problem definition is the result of a reasoning process conducted by the researcher in order to translate the phenomena to be examined into a (scientific) researchable (and relevant) research problem. Therefore, a problem definition is the researcher's 'product', as he creates a certain formulation in order to define the problem from his perspective (based on his present knowledge and experience). It is important not to forget that a problem definition often contains quite some symbolism[15] and tends to be rather abstract. A problem definition consists of both a research objective and a logically derived research question; these precisely establish what needs to be examined and why and under which (pre) conditions it should take place. This question is often based on complex reasoning about phenomena in the organisation guided by theoretical notions. These derive content and create meaning given its relevant context.

---

[15]Symbolism here refers to the fact that the problem 'stands' for something in the organisation. It is a framed and labelled phenomenon referring to e.g. 'bad management' or 'to much bureaucracy' or 'incompetent people'.

Box 1.6: Presenting Your Research
Prepare a short presentation of your research so far (maximum: 5 min). In this presentation you should address:

(a) What the research is about (perhaps you can tell us something about the occasion and the context?)
(b) Which question(s) you aim to answer by doing this research?
(c) Why is this of importance?
(d) What kind of research you want to conduct to answer that question?
(e) If there are any important conditions you have to take care of

A problem definition has a dual function. On the one hand, it is an important way to achieve synchronisation between the client, the university (tutor or supervisor of the research project) and the researcher (student). A problem definition is also a 'vehicle' creating a possibility to communicate about what is perceived as the problem. It helps to shape and focus the research. The research objective states what is to be accomplished by the research and for whom (or with whom), as well as what the probable result will be (knowledge, a model, suggestions for improvement, a change) and why this is relevant (for those involved). The research question establishes the main question, outlining the research objective in a comprehensible way. This means, for instance, that the research questions need to relate to an existing theoretical body of knowledge or an established conceptual model. The research question is an important starting point for deriving (logical) sub-questions. Sub-questions provide the specification of the central research question in the sense that they need to be answered in order to provide the answer to the main research question. Formulating just the necessary number of sub-questions is a difficult task. As a rule of the thumb, stick to a maximum of three; in general more questions can't be answered. Possible methods and techniques (see also Chapter 2) also have a dual function. On the one hand, they are used for collecting and analysing various data deemed necessary to answer the research question. Simultaneously they should adhere to any pre-conditions stipulated in the research, such as the explicit conditions the client demands regarding the design and performance of the research and the use of the results.

It often takes the researcher quite a long time to produce a crystal-clear problem definition (and a logically derived research question and -objective) at the start of the research. Pre-conditions are regularly overlooked at this stage. In order to test whether a problem definition is a 'good' one, it can be assessed according to the following three criteria: (a) relevance, (b) effectiveness and (c) researchability. It is wise to examine the tentatively developed problem definition more then once against these criteria. They can be elaborated with the help of the following checklist:

Box 1.7: Checklist Problem Definition
Please consider each of the questions below before moving ahead with your research.

1. Does the problem definition provide a reliable argument for the research goal?
2. Is the problem definition clearly related to the problems of the client (and) (or) the organisation (and) (or) the context?
3. What sort of relationship is there between the people involved with the problem (creators, sponsors, solvers and those who are concerned with the problem)?
4. What does the answer to the (research) question yield for the organisation concerned?
5. Are the (first) ideas about the design, structure and realisation of the research such that they actually contribute to answering the question?
6. Is the research feasible given the environment in which it needs to be realised; are required sources accessible?
7. Is it well-founded research, that is to say, is clearly, completely and precisely indicating what is being questioned and where, and is it mutually consistent? Adopted from De Leeuw (1996)

1.8 The Position and Role of the Researcher

A logical and inevitable aspect of the requirements that are applicable when doing applied research is that the results need to fulfil the demands of the world of science on the one hand, and the more pragmatic demands of the organisation, on the other. Both want to be able to do something with the findings – yet what they want to do can be quite different. The requirements are certainly not unique and the researcher will need to justify his approach taking these two different fields of interest into account in his approach to the research. In order to live up to these demands the research will need to be designed properly, which means it needs to adhere to a systematic and controllable structure. At the same time, the results of the research will need to be such that the knowledge can be understood and implemented in the organisation that provided the assignment. We do not deny that under certain circumstances living up to two expectations can lead to a dilemma for the researcher.

Box 1.8: Discussing what Constitutes Good Research
Discuss the following questions:

(a) Who decides in your case what is *good* research?
(b) How can the knowledge that the research produces be used and by whom?
(c) Who is the owner of that knowledge?
(d) Who can and may use that knowledge as well (and under which conditions)?
(e) What are (and what can be) the (other) functions of the research?

Naturally, the researcher has his own ideas and opinions about the research, the assignment, the organisation and... himself. He cannot be considered a sort of machine without any opinions or standards, or a person who conducts research without any interpretations, emotions, insecurities and preferences. Whatever these opinions may be, it is valuable when they are included in the preparation, realisation and assessment of the research.[16] In the end, after all it is the researcher who is personally confronted with the demands of the company and the (academic) institute. This requires integrity, in order to be able to deal objectively and coherently with his and other people's points of views, opinions and insights. The tension area arising owing to the various demands placed on the researcher during his work is visualised in Fig. 1.1

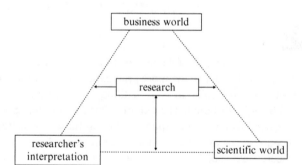

Fig. 1.1 The field of research

---

[16]Navigating between these different demands from various stakeholders might easily lead to tricky dilemmas for the researcher; we have noticed that. The fundamental issue addressed here are the ethics of *correct* or *good* research. Principles involved are e.g. respect for persons, informed consent, beneficence, anonymity and confidentiality. See: Beach, D. (1996). *The responsible conduct of research*, New York: VCH or Kimmel, A. J. (1988). *Ethics and values in applied social research*, Thousand Oaks (CA): Sage Publications.

1.9   What is Methodology?

In a book that deals with methodology, you may feel that surprisingly little has been said about the subject up to now. The previous section described the course the researcher follows when starting a research project – a course that has produced more questions than answers so far – you must have noticed. What has been brought to light is that research starts with an open or closed question. This initial question forms the basis from which to elaborate a problem definition and to decide on the research goal – and question. How you can turn that theoretical problem definition into a practical form of research – and put together a *research design* – has not been discussed yet. This is what the rest of this book is about. All we would like to bring to the fore in this last paragraph are some general remarks regarding methodology.

Methodology[17] is, broadly speaking, the way in which a researcher conducts research. It is the way in which he chooses to deal with a particular question (which may consequently result in a problem definition). He also has to consider the way in which he is going to deal with the (people of the) organisation and establish his overall approach, by choosing how he wishes to conduct the research. The researcher may decide to create a questionnaire and send it to people in the organisation. He can also opt to work in the organisation (literally) in order to be able to observe the organisation as he collects data. Which method he selects depends both on the nature of the question, and on the view of what he considers (implicitly or explicitly) to be 'good' research. This amalgam of (scientific) considerations and contextual conditions are shaped by personal preferences, previously referred to as the researcher's *basic approach.* There are two clear categories:

- The first researcher conducts research in the organisation by means of a well-defined research question. This question often appears to have a closed character. This form of research is characterised by research activities that are accomplished in a definite order of rank.
- The second researcher conducts research 'with' the organisation, often based on an open question. What needs to be examined exactly, let alone how it should be done, is not determined in advance. The most important element of research based on an open question is the 'search behaviour' of the researcher. Research questions are used as 'road signs' leading from one place to the next.

---

[17]With all due respect to many others before and after him we think the one and only Godfather of methodology was René Descartes (1596–1650). In 1637 he wrote a slim manuscript called "Discourse on Methods". In this landmark book (published in Latin in Holland give the limited freedom of expression he had in his own country at that time) he proposed a four-step method. These steps are based on intuition, deduction, enumeration and reporting. It takes little effort to recognise much of our contemporary approach to research in this method. By the way, the book is still available in any good book shop. Quite remarkable: a 400 year old bestseller. For more information please visit: http://www.iep.utm.edu/d/descarte.htm.

Naturally, it is possible to pursue an approach that combines elements from both of these perspectives. We will elaborate this during the second Interlude halfway through this book. It may also be the case that in the course of research the nature of the question changes, so that a completely different basic approach is demanded of the researcher. Dealing with this situation in a clear, transparent and justifiable way requires a clear methodology; it requires a starting point, direction, specific action plan (methods) and an appropriate technique for collecting and analysing the data. What makes it possible to deal with all these aspects is discussed in detail over the next chapters.

1.10   Chapter Summary[18]

This chapter introduced the main topics of this book.

- Conducting research entails looking at reality. This 'looking at' is a problematic task; there are just as many interpretations of reality as there are people (or so it seems sometimes).
- Conducting research within the framework of this publication puts an emphasis on applied research; it is research asked for by a company or organisation. The researcher who conducts applied research uses the 'rules of the game' and 'tools' of scientific research.
- When a question has been raised, it has to be established where a problem exists in the organisation and who the stakeholders of the problem are.
- Researchers translate problems into research questions; the distinction between 'open' and 'closed' questions was, therefore, introduced.
- In line with the nature of the question, the issues of problem definition, research question and research objective were briefly outlined.
- Attention was also paid to the role of the researcher in the research and, in particular, to his basic attitude when conducting research and the dilemmas that might arise.
- At the end of the chapter, a provisional description of the term 'methodology' was introduced and two basic approaches were described, entailing conducting research either 'at' or 'with' an organisation.

These topics will be covered in more detail in the following chapters of this book. In the next chapter we will focus on the notion of 'methodology'.

---

[18]At the end of each chapter (except the last one) you will find a summary of the salient points. If you lack time or just need to refresh your memory you can start by reading all these summaries one after the other; it will give you a pretty good impression of what it entails to design an appropriate methodology.

References

As you will notice throughout the book we have included some Dutch references. For us these references represent corner stones of our 'body of knowledge'. For the sake of readability we have decided not to quote abundant sources. In the following list a limited number of references are provided for the topics covered in this chapter. We do not pretend that this list is complete. For each of the following chapters there will be a similar overview. However, at the end of the book, after the Glossary a more comprehensive list of literature is provided.

Collis, J. & Hussey, R. (2009). *Business Research: a practical guide for undergraduate and postgraduate students* (3rd ed.). New York: Palgrave McMillan.

Cooper, D. R. & Schindler, P. S. (2008). *Business research methods*. Maidenhead: McGraw-Hill.

De Leeuw, A. C. J. (1990 & 1996). *Bedrijfskundige Methodologie: Management van Onderzoek*. Assen: Koninklijke van Gorcum and Company

Doty, D. H. & Glick, W. H. (1994). Typologies as a unique form of theory building: towards improved understanding of modelling. *Academy of Management Review, 19*(2), 230–245.

Gill, J. & Johnson, Ph. (2002). *Research methods for managers*. London: Sage.

Gronhaug, K. & Ghauri, P. (2005). *Research methods in business studies*. London: Pearson.

Gustavsson, B. (2007). *The principles of knowledge creation: research methods in the social sciences*. Cheltenham: Edward Elgar.

Hallebone, E. & Priest, J. (2009). *Business and management research: paradigms and practices*. New York: Palgrave McMillan.

Maylor, H. & Blackmon, K. (2005). *Researching business and management*. Basingstoke: Palgrave Macmillan.

Pennink, B. J. W. (2003). Judging management research .www.pennink.nl/bjw).

Ruane, J. M. (2005). *Essentials of research methods: a guide to social science research*. Malden, MA: Blackwell.

Scott, M. (2007). *Developmental research methods*. London: Sage.

Thomas, A. B. (2004). *Research skills for management studies*. London: Routledge.

Van Aken, J. E. (2004). Management research based on the paradigm of the design sciences: the quest for field-tested and grounded technological rules. *Journal of Management Studies, 41*(2), 219–246.

Chapter 2
The Essence of Methodology

Abstract This chapter explores the notion of 'research methodology'. The essence of methodology is structuring one's actions according to the nature of the question at hand and the desired answer one wishes to generate. Exploration is illustrated by means of a 'Box of Bricks' elaborated for closed and open questions. This exploration is structured with the help of the 'Research Pyramid' which consists of four levels: research paradigms, research methodology, research method(s) and research techniques. This Pyramid provides the structure for a concise introduction to 'quantitative' and 'qualitative' research. The chapter concludes with some remarks on research design. Like the introduction, this chapter should be regarded as a mandatory chapter for anyone engaged in setting up a research project.

2.1 Introduction

Almost every student associates 'methodology' with drawing up a research plan. In educational practice, this is often limited to writing a questionnaire, collecting a limited set of data and, then, learning to apply some rudimentary statistics. This idea is obviously naïve and incorrect. However, it may possibly be a correct expression of the (implicit) perspective of what research is for the average group of students. This perspective is further strengthened by the terminological confusion about the word methodology and its underlying connotations. Terms such as 'methodology' and 'method' are often used arbitrarily. This can lead to a sort of methodological potpourri. Subsequently, one seldom hears questions asking, for instance, what a certain methodology has to do with a certain type of research, what the nature of the question is and what (core) theoretical perspectives are used to explore and conceptualise the issue at hand. As a result, the importance of defining the nature and possible contribution of a specific kind of research is often ignored. It is not surprising that in many studies – directed either at regular students, teachers or doctoral students – methodology forms a difficult, and preferably avoided, subject of conversation. That is a pity, to say the least. In academic life in general

J. Jonker and B. Pennink, *The Essence of Research Methodology*,
DOI 10.1007/978-3-540-71659-4_2, © Springer-Verlag Berlin Heidelberg 2010

or at least in carrying out a decent piece of research, proper and transparent choices are the key to success.

In this book, methodology is regarded as a kind of 'action reading' or more precisely as, an 'action repertoire'.[1] Action reading means: preparing a type of repertoire, based on a set of premises, (theoretical) considerations and practical conditions, according to which the researcher structures the logic of his research given the question he wants to answer. An implicit yet important assumption here is that the researcher should be able to justify the reasons for this choice of a specific (research) approach and make sensible choices based on the different requirements of a particular question. There are *methodologies* that steer action for all kinds of activities (both mentally and literally) inside as well as outside organisations (see also Chap. 6); so a methodology is not only about doing research, it is about *acting*. Action reading that centres on doing research helps the researcher to systematically elaborate his approach using an 'open' or 'closed' question (see Chap. 1). This '(re)search behaviour' is guided by self-evident 'facts', notions, beliefs and premises the researcher (implicitly and explicitly) uses to 'frame' how he can come to know the world. Simultaneously, a connection needs to be made to the specific 'world' – or context – in which the problem or question occurs. Obviously, the central question is 'how' the researcher will shape that behaviour. What choices does he have? In which way do these choices play a role in his search behaviour? Where and when are his choices expressed? To make this connection and provide guidance we developed the 'Box of Bricks of Research' which is introduced below (see Fig. 2.1).

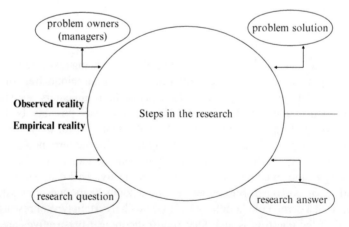

Fig. 2.1 The box of bricks of research

---

[1]We have chosen the words 'action reading and -repertoire' given the fact that the English language does not have an equivalent for the Dutch (or related German) 'handelingsleer' which, literally translated, means 'doctrine for acting'.

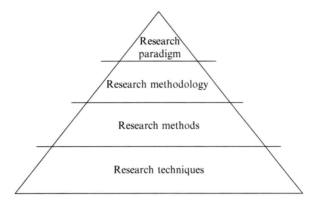

Fig. 2.2 The research pyramid

Direction on how to define appropriate (re-)search behaviour is furthermore supported by means of the 'Research Pyramid' (see Fig. 2.2). This pyramid is composed of four 'action' levels: paradigms, methodology, methods and techniques. On each of these four levels choices need to be made. One can consider this pyramid as a (logical) chain of interconnected events ranging from rather abstract (on the paradigm level) to very concrete (on the technique level). Moving from top to bottom through this pyramid leads to an elaboration of the research question based on clear-cut arguments leading to specific choices. Making choices on these four levels is steered by both the nature of the question and the researcher's 'basic approach'. This 'basic approach' can be typified by the distinction between 'knowing through the researcher's eyes' or 'knowing through somebody else's eyes'. The result when done well is a dedicated customised methodology for the research project. A fundamental premise here is that the researcher is in a position to manage his research process and can be held responsible for the choices made.[2] Given the fact that there is an infinite range of possible choices, it is in the end the researcher's method or reasoning that leads to a transparent and justifiable research design and the subsequent action.

2.2 Search Behaviour: From Problem to Answer

When the researcher starts his research his starting point can be described using the 'Box of Bricks'. There is a problem (think back to all the previous remarks on the nature of the problem and the process of problematising in Chap. 1). That problem

---

[2]For us methodology remains an exciting kind of 'Alice in Wonderland' experience. The sheer act of considering and making choices, understanding the underlying structure of the reasoning process: that is maybe what 'pure' methodology is all about. One rather important condition in all of this is that there is room to make these choices. Otherwise you can't be held responsible for the result. We will touch upon this issue again in Chap. 6.

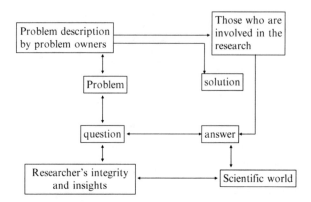

Fig. 2.3 From problem to answer

results in a (research) question demanding an answer. The answer is generated on the basis of research; on the basis of the researcher's deliberate search behaviour. This answer in turn creates the basis for the solution to a problem, although this will not always be the case. One might very well see this as a four-part 'problem-question-answer-solution' puzzle.[3] The line of reasoning is visualised in the Fig. 2.3.

This four-part 'problem-question-answer-solution' puzzle is complicated by its 'double context.'[4] Firstly, there are the problem owners who have certain ideas about the problem (see Chap. 1). Secondly, there are other parties (inside and outside the organisation) who are connected to the problem in various ways and have their own opinions (do not forget: make a stakeholder analysis if necessary and establish how important they are in terms of influence!). Finally, there is the researcher with his personal interpretation of the problem; an interpretation that changes over time. Yet in the end, it is the researcher who needs to provide a solid answer which meets both the demands of the research world, and is also relevant to the world in which the problem occurs.

The difficulty here is that to the problem owners the possible problem solution is not necessarily the answer to the question that is troubling the researcher.[5] Problem and question sometimes have their home in two different worlds, hence the double

---

[3]This diagram is our adopted version of what is generally known in the literature as the 'empirical cycle'. In Chaps 4 and 5 this cycle will be used in an inductive and deductive manner.

[4]This 'double-context' touches upon the problem of hermeneutics, the "art, skill or theory of interpretation, of understanding the significance of human actions, utterances, products and institutions, ... concerned with the theory and method of the interpretation of human action ... from the perspective of the social actor."

[5]Full-frontal we touch upon the manipulability of a problem. Problems can be used by people in organisations to generate additional means of exercising power – solving them is about the last thing they would like to do. Looking at this from a certain distance shows that problems have all kind of dimensions and are not necessarily always perceived from the analytical stance taken here. We cannot provide a 'solution' to this phenomenon, but at least warn you about it.

context. This double context consists of 'perceived reality' (by the problem owners as well as by the researcher) and 'empirical reality'; what the researcher 'sees' during the research that he is conducting. The researcher needs to navigate between those two worlds, or contexts. This implies delicate navigating between different demands and criteria, which continuously force him to make choices without knowing what the ultimate consequences are and if these choices are, thus, appropriate. It forces him into constant reflection on which steps to take in his research, steps that take into account how he looks at these 'worlds', how he deals with intermediate findings, how he chooses solutions. Making these choices is what structures his research. It is certainly not an easy task!

2.3 The Research Pyramid

It should be clear by now that once the researcher has identified the question at the start of a new project, he is confronted with a number of options he needs to choose from. If the choices are made properly, the research will be sound. However, the problem here is that often a researcher is not really aware of these choices, how they correspond and the fact that he needs to make many of these choices in advance in order to end up with a proper design. In order to help structure this often-difficult decision-making process the Research Pyramid has been introduced here.

The pyramid is composed of four levels. These are:

- The research paradigm: how the researcher views 'reality'. A paradigm is expressed in his 'basic approach'
- The research methodologies: 'a way' to conduct the research that is tailored to the research paradigm
- The research methods: specific steps of action that need to be executed in a certain (stringent) order
- The research techniques: practical 'instruments' or 'tools' for generating, collecting and analysing data

The key function of the pyramid is to help the researcher learn to consciously structure his approach to the research. The research will need to be designed in such a way that the researcher is able to justify his research. The assumption here is that the researcher will have to make his actions transparent. In order to be able to do so the researcher needs to reflect on his approach and plans, and try to find out what he feels to be 'good' research.[6] Obviously, the question is then whether his implicit perspective on doing good research actually relates to the question he has to

---

[6]The notion 'good' refers to criteria that can be applied from the different 'worlds' as introduced earlier. What is considered to be 'good' in the academic context is not necessarily so in the context of the organisation – and vice versa. Naturally reference is made here to validity, reliability, accessibility and so forth. See Chaps. 6 and 8 for further elaboration.

research. So, a first and important step in setting up a research is to reflect on one's basic research attitude and follow it up with corresponding (re)search behaviour. Once this is more or less clear, it is important to complete preparation by making deliberate choices regarding the methodology, methods and follow-up techniques. It goes without saying that this is often a difficult process. In the remainder of this chapter deals in detail with the different choices offered by the Research Pyramid and its four levels.

2.4 Basic Attitude Matching 'Search Behaviour'

The (implicit) way a researcher approaches reality and his research can be referred to as his *basic approach*. Premises and presuppositions regarding how reality can be known characterise this basic attitude. This implies that reality can be known in different ways, from different perspectives and with different purposes.[7] Usually, a basic attitude is called a paradigm. Gummesson (1999) describes it as: '... the underpinning values and rules that govern the thinking and behaviour of researchers'. Or it can be defined as: "... a term, which is intended to emphasize the commonality of perspective, which binds the work of a group of theorists together in such a way that they can be usefully regarded as approaching social theory within the bounds of the same problem" (Burrel and Morgan 1979, p. 23). Basically, a paradigm can be seen as a coherent whole of assumptions, premises and self-evident facts as shared by a certain group of professionals (consultants, researchers, teachers, managers, etc.) with regard to a specific (a) *domain of reality*, either (b) a *certain object or subject of research*, or (c) *the way in which research can be conducted*. As it is clear from this description, different kinds of paradigms can be discerned for different groups of people either in academia or in organisations. Paradigms can, thus, be considered very useful mental tools, frames of references that help people within a particular group communicate and understand each other. In any domain people pose paradigms in order to guide their acts and behaviour. Just think of nurses, doctors, accountants, consultants or yes, managers. Here a distinction will be made between *theoretical paradigms* and *methodological paradigms*.

A *theoretical paradigm* concerns the prevailing thought(s) about a certain research subject or object. In this case, the term *theory* already refers to certain existing insights and perceptions that consist of (validated) notions and terms and the way they are interconnected. 'A theory is an idea or set of ideas that is intended to explain something. It is based on evidence and careful reasoning but it cannot be completely proved.' Collins Cobuild (1987, p. 1515). Theory helps to observe and

---

[7]The question about how we know what we know or what we assume to be knowledge is covered by epistemology.

interpret reality and offers, whether justifiable or not, frames of explanation (or an initial impetus) for phenomena in that reality. Or in the words of Cooper and Schindler (2008), p. 51): A theory is '. . . a set of systematically integrated concepts, definitions, and propositions that are advanced to explain or predict phenomena (facts); the generalizations we make about variables and the relationships among variables.' Research cannot be done without theory![8] Our interpretation of reality and the phenomena under study always appear because we bring a kind of theory to that (empirical) reality. Any observed phenomenon is, thus, 'loaded' theory.

A *methodological paradigm* is specifically about research behaviour and can, therefore, provide indications about the way in which research should be conducted. A specific research methodology directs the behaviour of the researcher, but – conversely – the researcher may have a certain affinity with a specific form of research (no matter how unintentionally). Therefore, the (implicit or explicit) choice of a specific research paradigm is directed by the nature of the question respectively the phenomena to be examined, their context and the affinity of the researcher. This affinity, which we call basic attitude, is quite determining in setting up a research.

2.4.1 Basic Approach

Anyone who examines a problem will not start from scratch but with some kind of pattern, some assumptions and ideas in mind. The researcher will make an attempt to isolate phenomena which need to be examined in reality (e.g., "I'm conducting research on the value chain of this company."), either using an existing theory or theoretical notions (cautious initiatives). In this way, he aims to obtain insight into the way the phenomenon is functioning or dis-functioning. Each researcher, therefore, has knowledge (no matter how implicitly) about how reality is to be perceived in advance. This could be called a-priori knowledge. What is more important is that this knowledge also contains a number of criteria of what is 'good' and what is not. These are not methodological criteria but theoretical criteria regarding the phenomenon under research.[9] Here the focus is on the researcher's opinions (often unintentional) about the way the research should be conducted. These opinions are called *basic approach*. We distinguish between approach A and B.

---

[8]Just let this observation sink in for a moment. If reality cannot be observed without theory then any act, any observation even any reflection is drenched in theory; it cannot be made or pronounced without that theory. This is the ultimate consequence of the double hermeneutics we talked about earlier.

[9]So two sets of criteria are involved here: (a) one regarding the way the phenomenon under review can be judged (a priori) on the basis of available (theoretical) knowledge and (b) criteria regarding the way the research should be approached given the research question.

2.4.1.1 Knowing Through the Eyes of the Researcher

The essence of basic approach A is that the researcher can create an image of the (empirical) reality that needs to be examined in advance, behind his desk on the basis of existing knowledge, etc. Subsequently, this image will be given clear shape by means of a conceptual model that structures the remaining research activities (see Chap. 3). The researcher explores or tests through his research the extent to which the ideas that he has created about reality *beforehand* are correct; whether they are true or false. A core aspect of this approach is that a specific phenomenon in reality can be known a-priori on the basis of (already available) knowledge. This body of knowledge can be found in e.g., publications.[10]

2.4.1.2 Knowing Through the Eyes of Someone Else

The essence of basic approach B is that the researcher knows that he needs certain (sometimes vague) theoretical notions about a specific reality. Yet, it is the people in the perceived reality (the company) who hold the key to profound knowledge of that reality. He must therefore try – methodologically – to observe reality through the eyes of someone else. The researcher is able to discover that these two basic approaches – only methodologically typified here – point to concepts (and paradigms)[11] used for defining how we know reality.[12] In the context of this text it is how a researcher knows that he has discovered something about reality by means of his research. It would extend far beyond the scope and aim of this book to reflect upon the actual debate in this field of 'knowing' and 'knowledge' about reality, although interesting in itself. Still it would not make much sense to even try giving a short outline of this field here. The theory of knowledge is indisputably multifaceted. It suffices to provide a popular classification of the two central notions behind these basic approaches. Here this is indicated by the denominators positivism and constructivism.

---

[10]Just one little remark here. Using material from others is of course – when you start thinking about it – also a way of observing or coming to understand the world through the eyes of someone else. So the introduced distinction is less sharp then it might appear at first sight. Yet, for the sake of clarity we stick to these two basic attitudes.

[11]Please observe the confusing use of the notions of 'concept' and 'paradigm' here. Although we will elaborate on 'concepts' in the next chapter it is worth spending some time considering how these two are related. Do first need a paradigm to construct a concept? Or can we construct a concept regardless of the (underlying?) paradigm?

[12]The issue raised here is called 'ontology': ' . . . the theory of existence or . . . what really exists, as opposed to that which appears to exist, but does not, or to that which can properly be said to exist but only if conceived as some complex whose constituents are the things that really exist' (Dictionary of Modern Thought 1977, p. 608). Ontology relates to ' . . . our assumptions of reality such as whether it is external or a construct of our minds' (Jaspahara 2004, p. 93).

Box 2.1: Questioning the Basic Approach of the Researcher
There are two basic approaches. Basic approach A: Knowing through the eyes of the researcher. This implies knowing based on individual experience and test results.

Basic approach B: Knowing through the eyes of someone else. This implies knowing by hypothesizing and discovering.

Please consider for a moment what your approach is and if this approach corresponds with the question you are addressing in your research.

Please consider for a moment what your attitude is and if this corresponds with the question you are addressing in your research.

2.4.2 Positivism

The aim of applied research is to provide solutions to problems that occur in practice. Researchers focus on creating (re)designs and plans of action for these problems. Their approach is based on the belief that (scientific) action produces concepts that are useful. Most researchers are taught to deal with these problems during their studies by following a three-step approach: diagnosis, design and change. Firstly, create a clear problem definition, then design a solution and, finally, implement it. This often results in the development and implementation of a number of instruments and techniques: organisational 'recipes' that have to be mixed together carefully if the desired effect is to be achieved. An important condition is that the people who are involved in the research act upon these tools themselves. The fact that in practice it often appears that this approach does not work (or just to a limited extent) is attributed to people's resistance to change and the course alterations which take place during the implementation of the desired changes. Yet, the researcher can claim his innocence, because he handled the project in a methodologically correct way. The researcher decides on the best form of research for a specific situation using his expertise. He bases solutions on facts that are obtained by means of research he justifies 'scientifically'. It should be noticed that in many cases, books in the field of business research which predominantly focus on methodology do not even consider implementation as part of the research. This description, which should be interpreted with a mild smirk, is generally called 'positivism'. We are convinced that valuable research is conducted when the researcher also takes into account the implementation of the research results.

2.4.3 Constructivism

Applied research takes place in the complex environment of an organisation. People, systems, processes, procedures, culture, designs, attitudes, behaviour, rules, politics; everything is going on and changes at the same time. Everything is true or at least valid and results in a variety of problems. Whoever makes an attempt to examine an organisation, let alone tries to change it, will find that each group of people, each department or each location has its own characteristics, habits and rules. That is why each time we face a unique problem, one that is actually only understandable and solvable by reflecting on knowledge and experience gathered during the course of the research inside the organisation.

Employees who are involved in research constantly have to reconstruct their own reality and change it to adapt to the situation and to developments. There are no standard approaches, designs or concepts. At best, they can be of help in developing a kind of guiding notion in order to frame a situation. Examining reality from the outside hardly engenders any new insights into the actual state of affairs. True insight requires reaching an understanding of a situation, together with those involved, in order to develop 'theories' regarding the meanings and problems that occur in that situation and – in line with that – create solutions that are suitable, understandable and applicable. The researcher's role is to shape this process in such a way – together with those involved – that the uniqueness of the situation is done justice. This involves choosing methods that enable people to learn how to discover and change their own reality. In the course of the process, the researcher develops knowledge about the organisation, a learning process that is also shared by the people involved. In this context, the notion of validity obtains a complete different meaning. This concept is also known as constructivism.

Both interpretations can be elaborated in a number of ways. What is important here, though, is that the methodology and theory about knowing are explicitly linked. A connection created through the nature of the question, respectively the problem being examined and the way in which the researcher approaches the problem. It is impossible to develop a specific form of research prudently – let alone a specific kind of methodology – if any of the premises and assumptions regarding the phenomenon (subject or object) to be examined, are not taken into consideration. Choosing a specific *methodology* therefore is not something that takes place randomly. But then, what is methodology?

Box 2.2: Are you a Positivist or a Constructivist?
Form pairs and interview each other briefly in order to find out how the other person views reality: as a positivist or as a constructivist. Use open questions. Discuss the results of the interviews (preferably in a group) so that you can produce a broad overview of characteristics that belong to these two scientific concepts.

> **Box 2.3: Basic Approach to a Research Question**
> Look at the research question below and argue what your *basic approach*
> would be.
>   "We would like to find out how the workload is perceived in our hospital".
>   Discuss the outcomes of your considerations with others in the group (if
> possible) in order to get a clear understanding of the relation between the
> nature of the research question and your basic attitude as a researcher.

2.5 Methodology: Not a Map, But a Domain

Methodology is first and foremost associated with conducting research. The etymo-
logical and traceable meaning of methodology (deduced from Greek methodos =
meta hodos) is 'the way along which', in other words aimed at following a certain
route. In this case methodology implies: the way (or route) the researcher will need
to take in order to achieve a certain result (knowledge, insight, design, intervention,
solution). However, although a route (afterwards or on further consideration) can be
established by means of an intentional or unintentional starting- and finishing point,
it remains to be seen how the route is elaborated in-between.

Anyone who wants to travel from Paris to Rome can choose to go on foot, by
horse, by train, by plane or just take the car. What is more, the means of transport can
be changed along the way. Once on the road, unexpected developments (the train
does not go any further) can make you change your original plans and force you to
think of an alternative to continue on your way. This fundamental idea that 'there are
many roads that lead to Rome' indicates that there are choices within a specific
methodology. Ideally, these choices should lead to a similar result in the end.

Apart from the common use of methodology, the term comprises an additional
function for the researcher. Anyone who conducts 'good' research may sooner or
later be expected to justify the reasons for choices being made to his supervisor, the
client, people in an organisation, etc. Justification is only possible when you are
aware of the choices that you have made and how you have reasoned those choices.
You may need to justify these reasons to different stakeholders and explain why and
on the basis of which criteria and considerations you have dealt with certain
matters. In other words, you will need to be able to make your actions transparent,
thus, comprehensible showing alternatives, providing arguments and demonstrating
the reasons for what you have done.

Methodology implies '... a system of methods and principles for doing something' (Collins Cobuild 1987). As such a methodology is 'empty'[13]; it provides a
map, a starting and finishing point, but not the directions for the actual trip through a
certain area. 'Doing something' covers the methodology to travel, eat, pass an exam
or create change. This indicates that methodology is something completely normal

---

[13]This is a curious word here, 'empty'. It means that although the methodology provides cues for
how to act, it does not give specific instructions for any specific situation.

and convenient in all possible situations. Deliberately having a methodology for different situations, being aware of the construction of your own methodologies and how you will determine whether you have achieved your goal is, thus, very useful. Methodology does not simply mean 'conducting research', but in fact specifies way of acting in a particular situation with a clear goal in mind. We have already used the expression 'action reading' for this process before. Although it is very helpful to know what methodology is all about, its daily use is not the focal point of interest. This book concentrates on the use of methodology in conducting research. The basic objective is to show how to choose from different – existing – methodologies depending on the particular situation, problem or question. What is also important is the way the researcher himself deals – or wants to deal – with a particular research question. How do you view the question? What do you think when you look at it? Is it a question of gathering knowledge, of insight or of the way people view each other in an organisation? And what would you do about it? Only examine and then leave? Or would you provide recommendations for improvement as well? If so, what would your proposal be? Would you implement the proposal yourself or would you leave that to others? As a researcher you are supposed to deal with this question in such a way that you can explain how *you* have reached certain decisions.

Box 2.4: Defining Methodology

The word methodology is derived from the Greek 'meta hodos' meaning 'the way along which'. In more everyday language it means '... a system of methods and principles for doing something' (Collins Cobuild 1987). A methodology assumes there is a *logical* order the researcher needs to follow in order to achieve a certain predetermined result (e.g., knowledge, insight, design, intervention, change). Defining and defending the logic of this logical order is what methodology is all about.

Box 2.5: The Methodology Needed to Plan a Holiday

Imagine that you want to go on holiday. You have a (limited) budget, but you want to stay away as long as possible. You also want to see and experience a lot. You decide to go with a group of other people. Briefly describe how you determine what you will require to make this trip a success.

Box 2.6: Translating Your Intuition into a Methodology

You are visiting a company for the very first time. You instantly sense that there is a bad atmosphere. Now you need to translate your professional intuition into facts. Describe briefly *how* you could examine this situation. Please elaborate different approaches. Use a limited number of adequate keywords in a logical order to describe your approach. If possible: give a short presentation in which you logically present your considerations and choices.

2.6 Methodology and Method

Based on the preceding arguments, methodology can be considered to be action reading, i.e., what has to be done given a certain attitude, context, and concept in order to achieve a specific goal or destination. A methodology indicates the main path to the destination, but without specifying the individual steps. Methodology thus helps make the main outline of the approach transparent to both yourself and others (in academia and business). In this way, it functions as a compass, a beacon, a set of principles and *global* instructions. However, this does not mean that methodology prescribes what you should do (or not) in a specific situation or a particular moment in time. Such details entail methods and techniques. How one wants to fill in the approach with detailed methods and techniques is based on additional considerations, considerations which will depend on your basic attitude, the question at hand and of course the 'overall' methodological approach.

2.6.1 Methods

Methods (also often and rather confusingly called methodologies in many text-books) indicate specific steps (or actions, phases, step-wise approaches, etc.) that should be taken in a certain – eventually stringent – order during the research. It is obviously impossible to analyse data before it is available for example. Prior to the analysis you will need to consider the best way to collect the data. In this way, a method is adopted that can be compared to a railway timetable with arrival and departure times for all stations. Once the train has departed, it will pass all the stations in a fixed order. However, while it is unthinkable that stations will change places, methodologies for research are often not constructed quite as rigidly. However, the more concrete the methodology, the better the result.

However, the more open a question the more freedom the researcher has to create his methodology. Moreover, various aspects will play a role depending on the situation (contextually or organisationally). What access do you have to existing or new information, to data sources? Who owns this information? Are you allowed to talk to people? Under which circumstances will these conversations take place? How about confidentiality and anonymity? How much time do you have for this research? What are the (implicit or explicit) expectations of the results of this research? Who will benefit from these outcomes and in what ways?

It is these kinds of questions that will occur before and during the research, which will partly provide direction to and shape the methodology you will use. Therefore, when you have to give your reasoning for the chosen methodology and methods it will appear that the context in which you conduct your research explicitly influences the final research design. It also becomes clear that the many issues at stake in your research (e.g., ethical, technical, contextual) can easily lead to sometimes almost unsolvable dilemmas. It is virtually impossible to solve these issues before the start of your research. Still what you can do is treat them properly and in a transparent manner while carrying out your project.

> **Box 2.7: Distinguish Methodology from Methods**
> You receive the assignment to investigate a hotel's staff's level of motivation. Consider, argue and describe briefly: (a) which methodology you will choose given the situation at hand and (b) how you will elaborate this choice into a specific method; which specific steps do you plan to take and in which order. Describe the results of this exercise briefly. Reconsider and criticise afterwards the logic of your steps.

2.7   Techniques: Thinking and Acting

Further elaboration of the methods within a specific methodology takes place in choosing *techniques*, also referred to as 'instruments' or 'tools'. It is a matter of technique when the researcher strives to achieve specific goals on the basis of experience, rational consultation, scientific knowledge, calculations and the like. It involves applying a systematic way of working that includes established rules, regulations and procedures as a means to achieving the final goal(s).[14] Techniques can be understood as concrete instructions for acting that have an explicit, compelling and prescribing character.

Although it seems possible to clearly define techniques, it is less easy to indicate what the term really means. Technique roughly implies something like 'ability' or 'experience', which is expressed in a specific form of 'acting' instruction, but also in 'the specific way a specific issue is considered'. Taking a closer look, it can be established that there will always be one form of technique available for something, no matter what you examine. In order to recognise the nature of specific techniques it is useful to proceed by means of a classification. First of all, a distinction can be made between 'action techniques' and 'thinking techniques'. Action techniques are techniques that concern the practical actions (or activities) of people. This kind of technique we use throughout the day when making coffee, opening the door with a key or riding a bike. Acting techniques within the frame of doing research are, therefore, no more or less then a specific category of technique. Thinking techniques are techniques that classify thinking activities. Thinking techniques help to properly structure thought as well as obtain insights into the way one could think

---

[14]It might be good to state clearly that the same goal – or goals – can be achieved via different means and routes. We touch here on the philosophical debate regarding *teleology*, a notion derived from the Greek telos, 'end' and logos, 'discourse', the science or doctrine that attempts to explain the universe in terms of ends or final causes. Some also call this in a different setting the issue of *equifinality*: the fact that the same result can be achieved through different means.

about a certain subject.[15] Thinking techniques are therefore more theoretical by nature; they are also methodological in the sense they indicate 'a way along which to think'. Action techniques point to a certain goal in (organisational) reality that an individual wants to achieve by means of his actions.

The preceding examples are based on the conviction that the researcher has the ability to deliberately choose a certain (set of) technique(s). This would imply that an *intentional* choice is involved. Intentional means that a specific technique is chosen on purpose, with a clear-cut role and function in mind, knowing what the function of that technique is. Precisely by choosing this technique the researcher expects to achieve the desired result fast and efficiently. This implies that the researcher knows beforehand what a specific technique (or combinations of techniques) can and will deliver when applied. Choosing a specific technique, therefore, is normatively steered. The user of the technique has formed an idea of the effect that the technique will have if it is used. No matter how implicitly (apparently unintentionally) used, it is a question of the presumed relationship between a certain technique and the objective the researcher wants to achieve by using it. This links techniques to specific goals. Given a certain situation or question there is a potential supply – or domain – from which a researcher can choose his techniques. Furthermore, he can use the same technique (if need be combined with others) at different moments during the research. Here we are faced again with the principle of equifinality: similar techniques can be used at different moments and in different situations, either as complementary or fixed techniques in the process.[16] Which choices will be made at what moment depends on aspects such as the type of situation in which the researcher needs to operate (context), the course of developments in that situation (process) or the influence respectively the effect of certain (previous) actions by the researcher and/or others in that situation.

The choice for a certain technique (or set of techniques) is guided by:

(a) Norms and criteria
(b) Personal preferences
(c) The principle of equifinality
(d) Context
(e) Internal and external developments

---

[15]In philosophy this is known as the 'double hermeneutics': one can think in a certain way and think about the thinking itself. We have seen a similar issue previously when talking about the nature of knowledge and more in particular the way we know what we know or when we try to determine what it is we know. Here the ontology issue gets mingled with the hermeneutics. Please check if this could be the case in your work in progress.

[16]We refrain here from elaborating what the possible *causality* is between choosing specific techniques and how this causality might develop while applying them in carrying out the actual research process. Let's stick to the observation that using a specific technique in a specific situation alters *by definition* that situation, even if it is only for a short moment in time. As such it is an *intervention*. When using a series of techniques – either simultaneously or subsequently – this interventional 'side-effect' will be reinforced – be it in a negative or positive sense.

Given the limitless opportunity to apply similar techniques at different times and with different purposes in mind the result in (no matter what) practice is a contextualised amalgam of different techniques.

> **Box 2.8: Understanding the Notion of 'Technique'**
> Verify the technique you use for the following situations: (a) lighting a match, (b) making coffee, (c) taking a right or left turn while driving the car and (d) interviewing a person. What can you say about the nature of these various techniques? Are they all the same? If yes: what do they have in common. If not: what makes them differ?
> By the way: in Chap. 7 you will find much more on techniques.

> **Box 2.9: Preparing a Talk**
> You receive an assignment to provide a talk of 15 min about the role of 'business alliances' for entrepreneurs of small and medium enterprises. Leave aside the *content* of your talk for now. Instead indicate: (a) the context of your talk, (b) possible choices you have in preparing it and (c) norms and criteria you – or your audience – are using. Craft a little design for your talk based on the outcomes of these considerations. Then sit back and ask yourself: (d) how you could have done this differently and (e) if there are other developments that can affect your lecture and what you will do if these developments occur.

2.8 Data Techniques

Techniques for doing research indicate how the researcher can either *think* about his research or carry out specific *actions* in that research. To create a proper research design one needs to use both in an iterative way. Thinking about one's research has everything to do with paradigms and methodologies – that should be clear by now; they provide the means to structure the research thinking. Acting techniques are the researcher's 'tools'. They shape and guide the way in which data[17] are generated, established, classified and analysed. Data involve all the information the researcher collects during his research. Techniques for collecting data are used within the framework of certain methods. This may regard data that is deliberately generated (e.g., answer scores of a questionnaire) or data that already existed (collecting a company's annual reports for the last 3 years). Data can be classified based on its nature. A distinction can be made between *linguistic data* (e.g., transcription of a conversation), *numerical* (in figures) *data* (e.g., a company's profit and loss

---

[17]Data are considered to be 'raw' information, usually in the form of facts or statistics that you can analyse, or that you can use to do further calculation (Collins Cobuild Dictionary 1987, p. 357). Or: facts (attitudes, behavior, motivations, etc.) collected from respondents or observations (mechanical or direct) plus published information (Cooper and Schindler 2008, p. 82).

account) and *visual* data (e.g., drawings, pictures, photos, rich pictures, etc.). It is common for similar techniques to be used although different methods and methodologies are being used (Rose 2001). We distinguish six types of data:

- Data type 1: existing numerical data
- Data type 2: newly generated numerical data
- Data type 3: existing linguistic data
- Data type 4: newly generated linguistic data
- Data type 5: existing visual data
- Data type 6: newly generated visual data

Depending on the choices that have already been made with regard to methodology and method the researcher can choose the technique that fits the nature of the data he wishes to obtain. In principle, four types of techniques can be distinguished:

- Techniques to *generate* data
- Techniques to *register* data
- Techniques to *classify* data
- Techniques to *analyse* data

An example using these techniques is provided below.

In a first step, the researcher chooses to make use of interviews, which is an 'action technique' that results in newly generated linguistic data. He can then decide to analyse the data by means of 'turns' based on sentences, which is a thinking technique aimed at classifying and analysing the information. After the analysis of the first series of interviews it may be necessary to repeat the procedure again; the same action technique is used once more. Then, based on the outcomes of the first round of interviews the researcher can choose to conduct the second series of interviews using a more 'open' approach. In this example the researcher has chosen to ask as few questions as possible to enable the respondents to interpret them as broadly as possible. The researcher applies a technique in a double sense: allowing himself to generate outcome he cannot foresee while at the same time applying a technique which encourages the respondents to think. By choosing this technique the researcher shows that he does not want to steer the way the data is structured. In his preparation he has also paid attention to the fact that the questions themselves are not directive. The way the researcher records interviews, for instance by means of a tape recorder, is a technique in order to collect data. Once recorded, choices have to be made regarding the way the data should be classified and analysed. The act of classification can take place on the based of a deliberately chosen thinking technique such as sentences, words, actors, turns and others. Considerations for choosing a specific classification technique is normally based on the assumption that the researcher wants to extract a certain meaning[18] out of the collected data. Finally, choices have to be made regarding the way data will be

---

[18]A definition of the meaning of 'meaning' is "the customary significance attached to the use of a word, phrase, or sentence, including both its literal sense and its emotive associations."

analysed that is, how the collected 'raw' data will be turned into a whole that makes sense. Classifying and analysing data are, thus, both techniques that will manipulate the original data. It is the researcher who will shape and guide this process of manipulation based on his theoretical notions, skills and assumptions regarding the outcomes he is looking for.

It is assumed that the researcher is able to choose more or less consciously between all the possible techniques he can use in his research (see Chaps. 4 and 5). In this choice, considerations about thinking and acting will irreversibly play a role. The decision to choose a certain technique (or set of techniques) then needs to relate to the chosen method and methodology. It is clear – though not obvious – that the chosen techniques, methods and methodologies are supposed to be consistent with the paradigmatic presumptions. Last but not least, all considerations, premises and choices need to pertain to the matter in question. What is more: the nature of the question should be the starting point.

2.9   The Distinction Between Qualitative and Quantitative Research

All the previous considerations lead to yet another issue. In the corridors of many universities the distinction between open and closed questions, between testing and discovering or between positivism and constructivism is briefly dealt with as the common distinction between quantitative and qualitative research or, even 'quantitative *versus* qualitative research'. Quantitative research is often regarded as being purely scientific, justifiable, precise and based on facts often reflected in exact figures. Conversely, qualitative research is often regarded as 'messing around', being 'vague', not scientific and not following a structured plan. Whoever conducts quantitative research adheres to tradition, works on distinct matters and produces reliable figures. On the other hand, anyone who informs his tutor about his intention to conduct qualitative research is likely to face criticism. In most cases, the researcher solves this dilemma by presenting it as a case-study design (see also Chaps. 3 and 5). Packaging it in this way is a generally accepted alternative in business studies and offers a solution to the possible methodological dilemmas that occur while choosing between qualitative and quantitative research. However, some questions remain unanswered. Just to name a few. What is the essence of both forms of research? How can they be distinguished from each other? What determines the choice for either one of them or for an intermediate form?

In the most extreme situation there is a tight relation between the different approaches A and B and the nature of the research question. Thus, research guided by an open question is guided by the attitude of knowing through the eyes of someone else. And research guided by a closed question is related to the approach in which knowing is developed through the eyes of the researcher and is based on conceptualising in advance leading hypothesis and testing. We think that this relation is not as absolute as stated here, but we will use this rather traditional distinction in order to align with mainstream methodological literature focusing on either a quantitative or qualitative research approach. This way, we can easily show two extreme positions and their consequences when carrying out research. In Chaps. 4 and 5 these approaches will be covered separately. Given the unique character of many of the questions that occur in organisations, deliberately choosing a specific research methodology – or an intermediate form – and elaborating it accentuates its importance.

2.10   Research Design

In the previous sections a great number of basic principles, assumptions and premises have been introduced and briefly discussed. Together they offer the researcher an almost unlimited number of combinations and thus choices, which may initially seem daunting. Anyone who has started research recently (or whoever finds himself in the middle of it) will often struggle to *design* his research properly. It is not easy at all to make the right choices at the proper moment without knowing what lies ahead. For us, a design describes a (flexible) set of assumptions and considerations leading to specific contextualised guidelines that connect theoretical notion and elements to dedicated strategy of inquiry supported by methods and techniques for collecting empirical material.

Still, the essence of sound research remains making clear choices that structure the research. This research behaviour is initiated by the (open or closed) question within a certain context (the organisation and conditions it puts forward). On the one hand, this question results in the search for – and elaboration of – a suitable theory or theoretical notions about the question, respectively the problem that has been signalled. In Chap. 3 we will handle this issue within the framework of constructing a conceptual model. On the other hand, the question results in the search for and elaboration of a research methodology that fits that question *and* theory. The choices that the researcher makes are on the cutting edge of question, theory and methodology – the design of research. Please be aware of the fact that in many textbooks research design is restricted to the methodology part. This leads in general to a design without taking into account the context, no elaboration on the nature of the research question and no connection with the chosen theory (see also Chap. 3 in this respect). A sound design should link these three!

At the start of research there is no design, because there is not enough knowledge about the question and a suitable theory has not yet been elaborated, let alone a deliberately chosen and defined methodology. In the course of his research, the researcher often discovers how the three 'building bricks' of the research design relate and connect to each other. However, this does not stop the researcher from deliberately and consistently searching for coherence while conducting his research, subsequently outlining it and then providing it with a clear contour. Conducting research does not only involve searching for theory in the form of

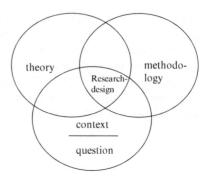

Fig. 2.4 Research design
related to theory,
methodology, question
and context

publications or collecting data by means of a chosen technique, such as an interview
or a questionnaire. Conducting true research requires the researcher to be in
continuous dialogue with himself and others (client, supervisor, respondents) in
order to slowly and gradually establish the coherence between these building
blocks. Conducting research demands constant reasoning. It requires the temporary
results of that reasoning to be explicit and well defined. If that has been accomplished correctly, it will mean the research is methodologically justifiable. This is
particularly true if the researcher is able to keep reporting comprehensibly about the
way he deals with the development of insights or testing of theory on the subject of
research in relation to the utilised theory about conducting research. Since many of
the issues raised here are not at all clear in advance it demands from the researcher
to keep a systematic track record of his research acts and of his deliberations in
handling them. It might be that in the end this track record provides the most
valuable insights because it will demonstrate transparently how the researcher has
handled the issue along the way Fig. 2.4.

2.11 Chapter Summary

This chapter has provided an explanation of the term methodology.

- The essence of methodology is establishing a path along which research can be
  directed.
- The choice of a methodology is framed by the nature of the question and by
  paradigmatic considerations with regard to 'knowing'.
- Two forms of knowing can be distinguished: knowing through the eyes of the
  researcher and knowing through the eyes of someone else.
- This distinction is subsequently elaborated in terms of positivism and constructivism.
- A methodology is clearly defined by means of certain (research) steps: the
  methods and techniques.

- Further finalisation of the method occurs with the help of techniques. Techniques concern the way in which data is generated, collected, classified and analysed.
- Choices with regard to methodology, method and technique can be denominated in terms of qualitative and quantitative research.
- Choices result in a research design

References

Arbnor, I. & Bjerke, B. (1997). *Methodology for creating business knowledge*. Thousand Oaks, CA: Sage.

Burrel, G. & Morgan, G. (1979). *Sociological paradigms and organisational analysis*. Hants: Gower Publishing.

Cobuild, C. (1987). *English language dictionary*. London: Harper Collins.

Cooper, D. R. & Schindler, P. S. (2008). *Business research methods*. Maidenhead: McGraw-Hill.

Creswell, J. W. (2008). *Research design, qualitative and quantitative approaches*. London: Sage.

Gomm, R. (2004). *Social research methodology: a critical introduction*. Basingstoke: Palgrave Macmillan.

Graziano, A. M. (2004). *Research methods: a process of inquiry*. Boston: Pearson.

Gummesson, E. (1999). *Qualitative methods in management research*. London: Sage.

Hallebone, E. & Priest, J. (2009). *Business and management research: paradigms and practices*. New York: Palgrave McMillan.

Marshall, C. & Rossman, G. B. (2006). *Designing qualitative research*. London: Sage.

Nagy Hesse-Biber, S. & Leavy, P. (2006). *Emergent methods in social research*. Thousand Oaks, CA: Sage.

Quinton, S. & Smallbone, T. (2006). *Postgraduate research in business: a critical guide*. London: Sage.

Ragin, C. C. (1994). *Constructing social research*. Thousands Oaks: Pine Forge.

Robson, C. (2002). *Real word research*. Oxford: Blackwell.

Rose, G. (2001). *Visual methods*. London: Sage.

Seale, C. (2004). *Social research methods: a reader*. London: Routledge.

van Beugen, M. (1981). *Sociale technologie*. Assen: Koninklijke van Gorcum and Company.

Chapter 3
Conceptual Models

Properties, Construction, Function(s) and Use

Abstract This chapter examines the use of conceptual models in applied research. First, some general properties of these models are outlined against the background of various definitions. Any model is based on theoretical assumptions so it becomes relevant to understand what theory is and the role it plays in constructing a model in your research design. Armed with these generic insights we then look at the role and functions of a conceptual model in designing research as well as at how it can be used in the context of a closed and open research question. In the final paragraph suggestions are provided for the construction of a model within the context of your own research.

3.1 Introduction

We have been quite easy-going so far regarding the use of the word 'model'. The word is quite common in everyday language and in management-speak. There are models for almost everything. We talk about business models, management models or specific categories such as quality models, stakeholder models or models for the value chain. Here we will restrict ourselves mainly to the properties and functions of models within the framework of research. In general a conceptual[1] model is nothing more than an abstraction of the way we choose to perceive a specific part, function, property or aspect of reality. It is a representation of a 'system' that is intentionally constructed to study some aspect of that system or the system as a whole (adopted from Cooper and Schindler 2008, p. 52). We share the opinion with many others that our (collective and implicit) perception of organisations is to a large extent shaped by precepts – a general rule intended to guide behaviour or thought – of systems

---

[1]It is time to say something about the word 'conceptual'. It means: 'based on mental concepts'. These concepts of the mind represent in a way paradigms and are, thus, fundamentally theoretical. The notion, furthermore, contains a reference to 'wholeness' – when you make a concept of something it implies it is a kind of encompassing or complete.

J. Jonker and B. Pennink, *The Essence of Research Methodology*,
DOI 10.1007/978-3-540-71659-4_3, © Springer-Verlag Berlin Heidelberg 2010

theory. An organisation is, thus, understood to be a complex system. The word 'system' means: an ordered entirety of elements. Systems tend to become complex when the elements interact in a variety of ways with each other as a result of specific and dynamic relationships (adopted from: Rüegg-Stürm 2005, p. 7). For starters, these demarcations and definitions might be useful in the context of research that is guided by an open or a closed research question. Before elaborating the nature of conceptual models in designing research it might be good to understand the characteristics of models in general and how they are related to theory a bit more.

3.2   Defining a (Conceptual) Model[2]

We are all very much acquainted with models, not only in everyday life but also in the natural and social sciences. Architects, consultants, designers, academics, managers and nurses all use various models. Most models serve to visualise ideas, bring to the fore key properties of a phenomenon and help to guide a specific pattern of actions or how things hold together in illustrating relationships. Basically, in the 'family' of so-called scientific models derived from a positivistic tradition hypothetical causal relationships are depicted, operationalised and then tested and verified. In the constructivist tradition models are not depicted up front but are often the result of a study. The model then provides a 'local theory' with regard to how people in a particular situation perceive and make sense of a configuration of acts and interactions. This model can then be put to the test. These models carry out principally different functions. In order to elaborate on this we will analyse the properties of models hereby drawing an analogy with maps.

3.2.1   Maps and Models

Closely related to models are maps. Any map is based on *signatures* representing certain properties of the depicted terrain. These properties do not have anything physical to do with the terrain itself, but are constructed, commonly agreed symbols, signs and definitions. They serve to help the user to reconstruct the 'terrain' in his mind and are aimed at fulfilling specific purposes. They help him to find his way. To this end a number of properties of maps are important here:

1. A map never represents a reality – it is a reconstruction according to purpose and task. Symbols used in the map are deliberately chosen and depend upon that purpose.

---

[2]This paragraph is inspired by the work of Johannes Rüegg-Stürm of the University of St. Gallen (Switzerland) who wrote a slim yet highly intelligent work on the European Quality Model published in 2005. This work called "The New St. Gallen Management Model" provides a neat theoretical and practical elaboration of this particular model.

2. The pivotal function is highlighting certain things *and* leaving other things out in other words: a map is an abstract reduction of a complexity *in* a perceived reality.
3. The usefulness of a map exists in what it omits. Since our world is infinitely complex, acting with a purpose in mind requires persistently disregarding certain factors in order to reduce this complexity.
4. The core of a map is to decide once – and not time and again – what is, or is not, important in a given context given certain problems, criteria and requirements.
5. Every map delineates (implicitly) the borders of perceived problems, thus, highlighting what deserves attention and what lies outside the scope of that problem.
6. A kind of 'one map fits all' does not exist. Maps are created or selected according to a goal and task to be accomplished – we naturally use different maps for different situations.
7. There are neither right nor wrong maps. Maps are more or less appropriate and functional according to a specific context and problem.

One specific point needs to be emphasised here. Despite all these properties, maps still do not tell us *what to do*. They provide no recipe for action. Only we, the users of the map, are capable of deciding which course to follow, which route to take. A suitable map can only facilitate this decision process. We are all familiar with what can go wrong in that respect.

3.2.2   Properties of Conceptual Models

It is evident that conceptual models have much in common with maps. Yet, it is interesting to see what the specific properties of a conceptual model are compared to a map?

1. They are verbal or visual 'constructions' helping to differentiate between what is important and what not. By definition models are based on choice.
2. A model offers a framework illustrating (logical) causal relationships between factors that matter (at least in the eyes of its creator). They, thus, promote 'sense making' or meaning in various situations.
3. Models serve to direct focus, thus, facilitating (organisational) communication which leads to speedier if not better understanding.
4. They create reality in the sense of collective understanding. Since they are based on (a) language derived from theoretical notions they offer access to these notions.
5. As a sophisticated linguistic (and) (or) visual construction it strengthens an organisation's ability to act collectively once understood.

We think models are to be understood as *contingent or contextualised inventions* illustrating a range of interrelated properties and postulating specific (causal) relationships considered to be important given a specific phenomenon or problem. Despite all these characteristics any model can break down and fail to fulfil its theoretical, methodological or empirical promises.

Models also tend to have blind spots. They do what they should do but still omit something important or even essential. This may be because the researcher did not detect what should have been included or purposefully excluded it due to a lack of professionalism. Models can also feign a false reliability. Finally, they have a tendency to replace reality – the model becomes an archetype of what is deemed desirable and in which reality has to fit. Given this criticism one could say that models are the fulcrums of academic 'disposables': they serve a certain purpose and should be thrown away afterwards. Whatever their properties, purposes or qualities, any model is constructed with ideas in mind. Ideas either held by the researcher (and the sources he uses) or by the organisational actors involved in constructing a model. Ideas are derived from theory.

3.3 Theory and Conceptual Models

It thus becomes appropriate to define what constitutes 'theory'. Key (1999) defines theory as: "a systematic attempt to understand what is observable in the world. It creates order and logic from observable facts that appear tumultuous and disconnected". A good theory would: "identify relevant variables and the connections between them in a way that testable hypotheses can be generated and empirically established" (Key 1999, p. 770, 317) or: "... a statement of relations among concepts within a set of boundary assumptions and constraints" (Bacharach 1989, p. 496). An important part of theory is the demonstration of relations between variables within a conceptual framework. Please observe the similarity here between what defines a model and a theory! A 'good' theory in the social sciences should meet the following criteria: it must be (a) falsifiable, (b) logically coherent, (c) operationalisable, (d) useful and (e) possess sufficient explanatory power in terms of scope and comprehensiveness. Ideally, "good theory should have both explanatory value as well as predictive value" (Key 1999, p. 770, 317). It must also be supported by a plausible or logical explanation to suggest how and why things happen (Labovitz and Hagedorn 1971, p. 925). A solid theory should also include the underlying logic and values that explain the observable phenomenon.

Conceptual models are inescapably based on theory or at least theoretical notions. Without this theoretical input, it is impossible to make a focused construction of a specific reality up front. Theory tells you where to look, what to look for and how to look. It is simply impossible to observe any aspect of reality, any phenomenon or problem without having a kind of theory in mind. That might sound quite conclusive by what we see, what we think is important, what we select for further inspection: it is all driven by theory. Without theory we can't make meaningful sense of empirically generated data or distinguish useful results. Without it empirical research merely becomes 'data-dredging'. Furthermore, the theory-construction process serves to differentiate science from common sense since a (in) direct objective of any research efforts is to create knowledge – fundamental or applied (also see Interlude I). This knowledge is created primarily by building new smaller or bigger theories, extending old theories and disregarding those theories that are not able to withstand the scrutiny of empirical research. Whatever question we ask, whatever data we collect thus reflects the impact of theory. Whenever we collect and analyse data, we are doing so in the light of underlying theories translated into frameworks, models or concepts (inspired by Foley 2005, p. 72).

So far this section must have provided ample arguments to enable the reader to appreciate the critical role of theory in any research. Theory helps to explain what is already known, what is missing and what the contribution of a research project can be. For now, a final distinction might come in handy: the distinction between what is called a 'grand' or overarching theory (such as Systems Theory[3]) and 'local' or small theories. Grand theories are sophisticated and (in part) tested constructs that explain dominant phenomena such as organisations or institutions. People in academia can spend a lifetime testing or altering such a theory. In this respect there are a number of grand theories 'competing' with each other. On the other hand there are local theories. The assumption here is that people – especially when working together in organisations – develop 'theories' about how to behave, what to do or what not to do related to the work at hand. Quite often applied research sets out to discover or test the construction of that local theory. Whatever the case depending on the nature of the question, selection of a theory linked to an appropriate methodology – or mix of methodologies – is a central issue. This is made the more difficult by the eclectic[4] use of theories in management sciences.

3.4 The Functions of a Conceptual Model in Designing Research

Maybe the previous two sections have been a bit abstract – or as we tend to say 'theoretical'. What will be done here is to bring together the different properties, assumptions and discussions, regarding models on the one hand and theory on the

---

[3]Please note that in this chapter we will talk about theory and systems theory in the same breath. Although the line to distinguish between the two is rather thin here we mean by theory (in general) '... an idea or set of ideas that is intended to explain something' ... 'which conceptualises some aspect or experience' (see Glossary). Systems Theory is a 'member' of the family of theory focussing on systems. This is particularly important here because we consider not only organisations systems but conceptual models also.

[4]Eclectic means: deriving ideas, style, or taste from a broad and diverse range of sources (source: any decent dictionary).

other, in order to outline the principal functions of a conceptual model in designing research. This will enable us to elaborate on the role of conceptual models either in a quantitative or qualitative approach.

1. The first function of a conceptual model is relating the research to the existing body of literature. With the help of a conceptual model a researcher can indicate in what way he is looking at the phenomenon of his research. The theoretical concepts used to construct the conceptual model introduce a *perspective*: a way of looking at empirical phenomena. Using scientific concepts provides the world with a specific order and coherence that wasn't there before conceptualisation. By using a (dedicated) model, he indicates which factors he will take into consideration and which not thus showing what he thinks is important. He then can start looking for (additional) literature providing arguments for his line of reasoning – hence the importance of adequate referencing. In doing so the researcher also connects his research with research results and theories of others. This enables justification on a theoretical level. This is probably the most important function of a conceptual model.

2. The second function is that building a model can be helpful in structuring the problem, identifying relevant factors and then providing the connections that make it easier to map and frame the problem. If done properly the model is then a truthful representation of the phenomenon being studied. Furthermore, the model will help to simplify the problem by reducing the number of properties that have to be included, thus making it easier to focus on the essentials.

3. A third and final function of a conceptual model is linking it to systems theory. This will allow us to make use of some important aspects of the characteristics of a 'system' as defined in systems theory (Checkland and Scholes 1990). In most systems theories a system entails two components: elements and relationships among the elements. "Understanding a system means: identifying the elements of the system, describing the relationships among the elements and understanding how the elements and relationships dynamically interact to result in different states of the system." (Northcall and Mccloy 2004, p. 27). There is clear analogy between the characteristics of a system and the previous definition of a conceptual model. For applied research we can make use of the following characteristics:

    (a) The first one is that in a system the elements are ordered in different *zones* from fundamental causes to outcomes. The elements of a system are classified and related in such a way that one element causes the second etc, thus, demonstrating *causality*. Please bear in mind that there is always the question here about the logic of the order itself and which relations are included in the system and which not. Once more this demands theoretical justification(s).

    (b) The second characteristic is related to the question of the *embeddedness* of the elements in the research. Embeddedness makes is possible to focus – or in systems terms – zoom in and out. In organisational situations it is rather handy if not a prerequisite to search for the *nature* and *degree* of embeddedness. *Nature* refers to how observable elements in the research are linked to one another. *Degree* points at stronger or weaker 'ties' between the phenomena. To observe the actual practice of embeddedness of phenomena in the research look for the *impact* on the different levels by zooming in and zooming out. We can use these notions of embeddedness (nature, degree and impact) in all kind of situations. While in the process of constructing a conceptual model it is important to be aware of these notions. Relating characteristics to different levels requires classifying these characteristics in a certain if not strict causal order. To do this in a responsible manner requires theory.

Box 3.1: Example of a Conceptual Model

Carrying out research on labour satisfaction and workload is done by asking employees how satisfied they are with their work, the actual workload, conditions, results etc.

The actual model consist of: Employees as the *unit of analysis*. The *properties* of the model consist of (assumed) perceptions concerning work, workload, context and satisfaction. Possible *relations* are between e.g. the perceived workload and degree of satisfaction – and it is possible to hypothesize other relations.

Box 3.2: Possible 'Side' Effects of Conceptualising

Sometimes the process of constructing a model and the presentation of it in an organisation can be sufficient to solve the problem. Managers give their version of the problems to a researcher and the researcher is able to translate these stories into a coherent model. The model then works like a mirror. Possible reactions are: "Oh if you see it this way than we know what to do". In managerial terms the problem is then solved since people can act upon the model they have created.

Box 3.3: Embeddedness

Imagine a project which involves comparing the results of several business units within a multi-nationals. In terms of embeddedness we can look at the various business units and at the level of (comparable) businesses. As a researcher we can pay attention to the level of the multinationals or business units or to both levels.

Box 3.4: Display of a Conceptual Model
In carrying out research on the diversity of mental models in management teams, the researcher chose to use three variables to construct his conceptual model. The (a) diversity in mental models between team members in a team, (b) the position in the organisation of a team member and (c) the gender of a team member. The causal assumption here is that the degree of diversity is caused by the other two properties. This is graphically displayed in the following scheme:

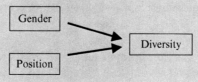

3.4.1 Question: Open or Closed?

The above demonstrates the role of a conceptual model in the context of research guided by a closed or open research question. Starting with a closed question the researcher gives a clear picture of which aspects are taken into account and which are not. Moreover he also indicates how these elements are related to each other and to the phenomenon being researched. A conceptual model then consists of units with attributes and relations between these attributes. In research, the attributes are referred to as 'concepts'. This model then guides the remainder of his research activities.

If the research is determined by an open question, the researcher cannot start with this clear picture. The use of an open question can be an issue of principle (and) (or) practice: the researcher does not know what is going on in the organisation and that is why he simple starts with an open question. It is not hard to imagine that in such a situation the construction of a conceptual model right at the start does not add value to the advancement of the research process itself. It is during the research process that the researcher hopes to detect which concepts and which relations might be relevant. The 'product' of research with an open question is therefore quite often a conceptual model.

Box 3.5: Different Starting Points for Conducting Research
If a researcher wants to find out how the treatment of patients in a hospital can be organised in *new* ways he can start by reading the existing literature but he also could start by going to a hospital and start with a series of open interviews (either individual or collective) with those who organise and carry out the actual treatment. Instead of looking at existing literature and concepts, the researcher chooses to start with some indicative concepts (called sensitising concepts). From that starting point he can develop ideas and knowledge about new ways of organising the treatment.

3.5   Role of a Conceptual Model with a Closed Question

Key to research based upon a closed question is the process of relating the theoretical model to the empirical reality.[5] Crucial is where the theoretical model and the empirical reality are related is when they are translated into observable constructs. This process is called "operationalisation". De Groot (1969) among others has given a detailed description of the process. Operationalisation is the process of changing a theoretical construct into a concept that can be "seen" in the empirical reality. This translation process is guided and supported by theory that can be found in the literature. Furthermore, this same literature can provide operationalised models developed and possibly tested by others.[6] To this first step we would like to add some features. The process of translation starts with reflection on the phenomenon that needs to be translated in empirically observable terms. Yet, theories alone are not enough; also reflection and the imagination of the researcher are necessary to come up with a good concept. Although the role of theory remains central, we think systematic reflection and academic imagination are essential to arrive at a translation into *indicators* that are measurable in the empirical reality. During a final step the indicators will be translated into a measurement instrument implying the constructing of a questionnaire with questions.

The process of operationalisation can be seen as the translation of a theoretical notion into measurable questions in several steps. Firstly, a definition of the concept (the construct as intended (De Groot 1969), secondly a translation into indicators and, thirdly a translation of each of the indicators into questions (the construct as meant). In all these steps the researcher has to decide how to use reflection, imaginisation and theoretical insights. Through the process new theoretical insights may be needed and of course previous ones may become obsolete. This may sound as if there is a kind of 'limitless liberty' during this process. This is only partially true since the researcher has to justify every step of the way. In Fig. 3.1 an overview of these steps is provided.

In terms of modelling we have to take into consideration the level of concepts and the level of variables (the concept as meant to be) and that can be quit complicated. Take for example three concepts A,B and C. In which C will be the concept to be explained by concept A and Concept B. When we add however now the result of the operationalization (e.g. Concept A ends up in two variables, concept B in one variable and concept C in two variables) we can see how complex the reasoning will be on the level of variables (Fig. 3.2).

Two additional remarks need to be made here. Principally within the context of research guided by a closed question the actual practice of the organisation – their

---

[5]Please remember that although we know it is philosophically doubtful to speak of an empirical reality we still do it for practical reasons.

[6]Characteristic of management literature in general is the abundance of a plethora of 'conceptual' models. We put the word conceptual between commas here because many of these models are based on the (practical) experience of the authors without any precise theoretical foundation. Wrapped in an attractive language and supported by some do's and don't this makes a first-class business case for consultants.

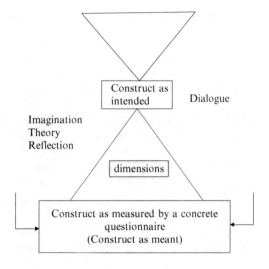

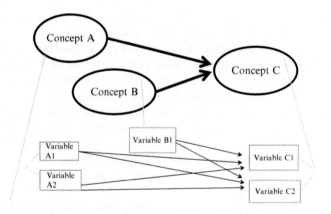

Fig. 3.2 Relations between concepts and variables

ongoing operations – will be kept outside this research process. Yet in applied research the researcher can ask for a kind of 'time-out' in which he can discuss with the people the usefulness of the model and the measurement instrument under construction. That is why we have added the term 'dialogue' to the figure. In a dialogue – could be more then one – he can verify and justify what he is doing. A researcher should at least think about this feature in designing his research. If he wants to introduce this feature Isaacs (1999) can be very practical.

The second remark concerns the construction of hypothesis. A hypothesis may be regarded as a statement of assumed empirical relationships between a set of variables (Ryan et al. 1992). It provides a description of expectations in such a way that in the formulated sentence no contradictions can be found and a relation with the empirical world can be made. By formulating these expectations, grounded in the literature and leading to the conceptual model, the researcher will test or falsify his expectations with the help of primarily numerical data. Developing a research design leading to testing hypothesis, two final comments should be made. The number of hypothesis that can be tested is limited. Furthermore despite the criteria of objectivity and reliability (see also Chaps. 4 and 8) outcomes cannot be generalised if the research is conducted in one – even embedded – case. This really requires a more sophisticated design.

> **Box 3.6: Operationalisation of the Environment of an Organisation**
> Take for example the operationalisation of the concept: the environment of an organisation. The researcher has to give a definition of this abstract idea. It might be wise to start by using an existing definition. If you do so you have to provide arguments why you has chosen this specific definition and not others. In the second step you will have to introduce some dimensions of this abstract concept. In the third step each dimension has to be translated in measurable terms. If the choice has been made for a questionnaire then 'measurable' means here developing questions for the specific dimensions. The result will be a questionnaire that will help ascertain the environment of an organisation.

> **Box 3.7: Construction of a Hypothesis**
> Take for example the following hypothesis: "Bad physical environment will have an effect on team performance". The researcher focuses on two concepts and a relation between the two concepts (and in order to test the first has to operationalise both concepts).
> The hypothesis can be made more precise by specifying the character of the relation. "Bad physical environment will have a *negative* effect on team performance". This does not mean that the first hypothesis is wrong. The second is simply more specific and has the advantage that after testing more specified conclusions could be formulated.

3.6   Role of a Conceptual Model with an Open Question

In the context of research guided by an open question the conceptual model plays a different role. Research guided by an open question leads to concepts and local theory emerging from the data in the process of the research (Bryman 2004).

Here a conceptual model can be considered as the constructed abstraction of how people (including the researcher) perceive local reality. The model then is a product of interaction and bargaining. The aim of producing such a model is (re-) constructed understanding between the actors involved which possibly lead to better communication about a specific situation such as actionable alternatives.

Instead of the more strict definition within research guided by a closed question in this context the 'definition' of a model can be described as "anything goes", the condition being that the researcher is able to justify his initial model. Models can be based on many underlying concepts, which as a consequence, result in a variety of possible relations. In the soft systems tradition of Checkland & Scholes, the main target of the model is to systemise the searching process in identifying elements and looking for relations. By making the initial model explicit, it is possible for the researcher to describe exactly which process the model will be developing. During the process the researcher will ask the people in the organisation to help him find out how the model should be changed so that it has a stronger relation with how they think the world look like. This means he will justify the process of research; steps to be taken and expected outcomes. The aim of the researcher is to develop his knowledge about a particular situation. This means that at the end of the research the original model will most probably need to be changed. Accounting for the changes in the model and the systematic comparison with the initial model will also be the result of the research.

The second characteristic of conceptualising is the role of 'concepts' used in the initial model. From the tradition of the grounded theory of Glaser and Strauss we see these concepts as *sensitising* (Strauss and Corbin 1998). These concepts will develop during the research; they are in a sense places of interest or road signs showing the researcher which way to go. A sensitising concept gives a general sense of reference and guidance to approaching empirical circumstances. Whereas testable models provide explicit prescriptions of what to see, sensitising concepts merely suggest directions along which to look. The hundreds of concepts we use daily – like culture, institutions, social structure, mores and personality – are not definitive concepts but are also just sensitising in nature (Blumer 1969, p. 148).

All kinds of data (see Chap. 2) can be used to develop the concept model guided by an open question until the researcher is convinced that the concept is fully elaborated. Data can range from observations to minutes of meetings, incidental talks, interviews on purpose etc. In the words of Glaser and Strauss the moment of *saturation* has been reached. This means additional data or analysis no longer contributes to discovering anything new (see Glossary). Data collection becomes entirely focused on the emergent model. "The researcher seeks evidence of saturation such as replication in the information obtained and confirmation of previously collected data." (Denzin and Lincoln 1994, p. 230). As the research progresses theoretical insights and connections between categories increase, making the process exciting since 'what is going on' really becomes clear and obvious (Denzin and Lincoln 1994). In hindsight it might be that the final sensitising concepts are totally different from the ones used at the start. Saturation remains a difficult yet crucial principle guiding research based on an open question. It is impossible to define in advance when, or on the basis of what kind of data, saturation will be achieved. Although applying triangulation is certainly helpful it is impossible to define the actual moment of saturation. It is only through his engagement in the actual research that the researcher will become aware of this. Justifying what he is doing in e.g. memos or a research diary (see Chap. 5) can be helpful in this respect.

> **Box 3.8: The Use of Sensitising Concepts**
> In carrying out research on leadership styles in different companies a researcher
> can make use of the existing literature and measurement instruments. But if the
> researcher wants to know in which way managers *themselves* talk and think
> about leadership he can use some elements of leadership as sensitising concepts
> and as starting points in the discussion. The managers will provide the descrip-
> tion of the actual leadership styles. Research starting with "Leaders are at the
> front of the battle – this requires a certain style" and "Leaders are the ones who
> guide others how to act" can be seen as sensitising concepts.

3.7 Constructing a Conceptual Model

What should a researcher do to construct his conceptual model? In this paragraph
we will give some simple yet not simplistic advice.

1. Maybe the best advice to start with is: make a quick scan of relevant models in a
   specific field. So, if your research is about general management models look for
   e.g. the 7S-Model, the Porter value-chain, the EFQM Model or any other model
   that fits the bill. If from the start your research is dominated by one specific
   discipline (e.g. economics, marketing and social-psychology) concentrate on
   relevant and current models in that discipline.
2. If you start with the (open) description of a (social) situation or the management
   problem a good question to ask is whether it is possible to provide an indication
   of how the people involved see the problem? And also to find out which label or
   heading fits the problem. Instead of asking which theory is related to the problem
   the researcher thus starts with a simple question. A good label enhances recog-
   nisability and makes it easier to broaden the description of the management
   problem as well as focus on a specific aspect of the problem. A subsequent
   question could be: 'Which theory can be related to the label?' In this way you
   can develop and sharpen your initial idea with the help of the label. For the more
   inexperienced researchers this can be very helpful. Instead of asking for theories
   in general a researcher is asked to look for a mini-theory that will help him focus.
3. The third tip is again simple. If you want to construct a model, simply start by
   making an image with a few concepts and depict relations. Instead of using
   (disciplinary) language that needs to be learned and forces you to express ideas
   in a specific way this imaging might help. Other tricks can be: make a list of all
   possible concepts and select a top five. Then in a second step make a list of all
   possible relations and then of a limited number, say three to five. Of course your
   decisions can be supported by existing theories.
4. The fourth piece of advice is that in the final conceptual model the researcher
   should use as few concepts as possible. In relation to that he also should use
   equally few relations between the concepts. Furthermore, these relations should

be one-sided demonstrating a specific kind of causality. At any cost circular arguments should be avoided!

5. In drawing a simple picture of the concepts in relation to each other the concept that will be explained will be put on the right side of the picture. The concepts that will be used to explain will be put at the left side of the picture. In between concepts can be placed between these positions, these concepts are called 'intervening concepts'.

6. Each of the concepts has to be operationalised (at least in research with a closed research question). In the picture this must be added below the concepts. At the level of operationalised concepts researchers make use of the term: variable for the operationalised concepts. At that level we make use of dependent variables (to be explained), independent variables (explaining) and intervening variables. An arrow from one concept to another, or variable to another variable is associated with phrase like: "this variable A explains the variance in the dependent variable B" and "concept A can be a cause for Concept B"

7. A seventh and final piece of advice is: do not let yourself be fooled by your own model. If you go back in this chapter we have warned you already that models tend to start living a life of their own. It looks as if that model dominates everything you do in your research. We have called that one of the blind spots. So, if you sense you are falling into this trap try to analyse very critically why this is happening.

All this advice will force you to simplify your ideas to the bare essence and ideas shaped this way are far easier to combine with, on the one hand, the existing body of knowledge in a specific domain and, on the other hand, existing tools and (statistical) techniques necessary for analysing the data generated by these models.

Box 3.9: A Label as a Starting Point in the Construction of a Conceptual Model

If you want to conduct research on how a management team operates, you could start with a label such as: "the different roles people can fulfil". This label can be related to existing theory, for example Belbin's role theory. The next step should be a specification within this theory. What is of interest in this theory for this specific research question?

If someone wants to do research on the development and introduction of a new product we could start with a label such as: "Business Development". Again the next step must be a specification.

3.8 Chapter Summary

• We started this chapter with a definition of a conceptual model: a conceptual model consists of units with attributes (concepts, theoretical constructs) and relations between those attributes and concepts based on theoretical constructs.

- The main functions of a conceptual model relate the research to the existing theories, focusing the research, making clear in which way the researcher is thinking about the things going on and providing the possibility to systematically pay attention to the embeddedness of the subject that will be investigated.
- When the research is guided by a closed question the focus is on the operationalisation of concepts in measurable entities leading to formulating a limited number of hypotheses.
- In the context of research is guided by an open question the focus is on choosing sensitising concepts and looking for relations that are relevant. The conceptual model emerges as a result of the research.
- Throughout the chapter particular attention was given to the notions of operationalisation, embeddednes and saturation.
- In the last paragraph some advice was given regarding constructing your own conceptual model. Look at what is already available and relevant, ask for a label instead of a theory, start with a simple picture and try not to fall into the trap of letting your model dominate your observations.

References

Bacharach, S. (1989). Organizational theories: some criteria for evaluation. *Academy of Management Review, 14*, 496–515.
Belbin, R. M. (1993). *Team roles at work*. Oxford: Butterworth-Heinemann.
Berkeley Thomas, A. (2004). *Research skills for management studies*. London: Routledge.
Blumer, H. (1969). *Symbolic Interactionism: perspective and method*. Englewood Cliffs: Prentice-Hall.
Bryman, A. (2004). *Social research methods*. Oxford: Oxford University Press.
Checkland, P. & Scholes, J. (1990). *Soft systems methodology in action*. Chichester: Wiley.
de Groot, A. D. (1969). *Methodology: foundations of inferences and research in the behavioral science*. The Hague: Mouton.
Denzin, N. K. & Lincoln, Y. S. (1994). *Handbook of qualitative research*. London: Sage.
Emery, F. E. & Trist, E. L. (1965). The causal texture of organizational environments. *Human relations, 18*, 21–32.
Foley, K. J. (2005). *Meta management*. Melbourne: Standards Australia.
Giere, R. (1991). *Understanding scientific reasoning*. Orlanda: Holt, Rinehart and Winston.
Isaacs, W. (1999). *Dialogue: the art of thinking together*. New York: Random House.
Key, S. (1999). Toward a new theory of the firm: a critique of 'stakeholder' theory. *Management Decision, 37*(4), 317–328.
Labovitz, S. & Hagedorn, R. (1971). *Introduction to social research*. New York: McGraw Hill.
Northcall, N. & Mccloy, D. (2004). *Interactive qualitative analysis, a systems method for qualitative research*. London: Sage.
Rüegg-Stürm, J. (2005). *The New St. Gallen management model; basic categories of an approach to integrated management*. Houndmills: Palgrave Macmillan.
Ryan, B., Scapens, R. W., & Theobald, M. (1992). *Research method and methodology in finance and accounting*. London: Academic Press, Harcourt Brace Jovanovich Publishers.
Strauss, A. L. & Corbin, J. (1998). *Basics of qualitative research; grounded theory procedures and techniques*. London: Sage.

Interlude I Conceptualising Methodology

"I think, this time … we really have a problem, don't you?"

"Hm, yes, I think I must agree but … can't we hire a consultant again … a good one this time?"

"You mean one that solves the problem and doesn't just send bills?"

"Something like that."

"Don't know if it is that kind of problem."

"Meaning ….?"

"Well, this time I think the problem is us. What we do. How we talk? How we decide? How do we treat each other behind our backs? That kind of things"

"Well, if you are certain, then we really have a problem."

A.1   Conceptualising Methodology

This first interlude focuses on the problematic nature of conceptualising a (organisational) problem with the help of methodology. It touches on a number of underlying issues, thus demonstrating the limits of any research design. As a whole it provides a critique of the measurability of organisational reality. The interlude is above all meant as 'food for thought'- not for solving problems. So, if the previous three chapters have left you dazzled by the kaleidoscopic nature of assumptions, paradigms and, yes, methodologies, do not read this interlude. But, if you are asked to provide a critical justification of your research design you definitely should (see also Chap. 8). We think this interlude is helpful in understanding and appreciating the content of the next two chapters on qualitative and quantitative methodology.

A.1.1   The Social Origins of Problems

The essence of applied research is and will be the researcher investigating a particular problem in an organisation or company that only occurs there and is, thus, of a unique contextualised significance. Essential to the kind of problems we address is that that they always occur in a social situation, in contrast to a laboratory experiment for instance. A social situation can be categorised in the following research 'areas':

- The *people* involved (the actors or stakeholders); who form the focus of attention in this research?
- The *actions* themselves; which kind of activities or events does this research focus on – decisions, operations, R&D?
- The *place* where it all happens; does it revolve around activities that take place at the headquarters or in the business units? Does it concern the observation of all possible situations or the same situation, but at different locations?

- The *time* when things happen; to what extent will attention (need to) be paid to time or moment? Is it relevant to observe something over the years or will the focus fall on the distinction between day and night?
- The used *'objects'* (and) (or) *knowledge*; does the problem revolve around the right use of certain rules, procedures, regulations at the proper moment and to what extent is this machine-related?
- The nature of the produced *goods* or *services*; to what extent might it be useful to make a distinction between tangible or intangible goods?
- The meaning and *intentions* of people's actions at a certain place and at a certain moment.

Anyone reading this will again realise that applied research focusing on problems is by definition embedded in the social side of the enterprise. It is people that experience a situation as problematic and subsequently name and frame it. Given this social nature a number of fundamental questions surface when it comes to analysing problems. Most of them have been touched upon in the previous chapters. Here we wish to address and elaborate some of them again thus providing 'food for thought'.

A.1.2   Instrumentality

It might be that your attitude when addressing problems – especially when doing research projects for the first time – is to accept a problem on face value. Something like: "... this is the problem as it is and this is where my analysis will start'. We previously outlined the idea that problems are human constructs. It is true that a certain reality can be problematic but it can also be the case that a specific reality is problematised with other purposes in mind, purposes that have nothing to do with the problem itself. Think of the person who protects his position by holding on to a (still to be solved but never will be) problem. Or the fact that as long as a problem is spoken about the person who possesses the problem receives attention. If that is the nature of the problem you will have to focus your research on the person since he or she might be a key part of the problem. Analysing this in a rational goal-oriented manner could possibly make the problem get even worse. In the end, the bottom-line message is quite simple: not all problems are constructed with the implicit desire to solve them. Some problems are created with totally different purposes in mind. Please be aware that your research is not about solving all kinds of problems in the world. You do not solve problems at random. Just addressing them in a scholarly manner is sometimes enough.

A.1.3   Intervention

The sheer act of announcing a research project is already an intervention in a specific reality. Even if you have done all your homework, the moment you announce that you are starting a research project in an organisation that organisation will change – albeit modestly and imperceptibly. Without necessarily pronouncing it people will have certain ideas, motives and expectations about the upcoming research event. 'What will he do?', 'Can I use this to some extent?', 'Will he see me and what will he then ask?', 'What kind of influence will this research have on my function?' or 'This is once more a demonstration of our incapable management – I will refuse any cooperation when it comes to it.' You can never be ahead of all these questions. The act of intervening through your research raises a real dilemma. And as with all dilemmas you are forced to make (difficult) choices – choices that are open to more then just one interpretation – that you then need to justify.

A.1.4   Measurability

The first two chapters have demonstrated the problematic nature of 'reality'. Still no criticism was formulated about the measurability of that reality. The term 'measurability' can be interpreted in various ways. On the one hand there is the notion of 'ability'. It refers to the level of professionalism of the researcher and his ability to carry out a decent piece of research. Is he capable of carrying out what he is planning to do in justifiable manner? On the other hand, there is the assumption that – if approached appropriately – reality is indeed measurable. It does no harm to question this second assumption. Indeed it is not complicated to measure the 'natural' conditions in a workplace: temperature, noise or humidity are all very measurable properties. What about notions such as the 'smell of the place', 'a hostile atmosphere' or even 'insufficient communication'? In order to make these notions measurable, it is necessary to make theoretical constructs (models) based on an interpretation. Even done properly in terms of reliability and validity the question still remains how measurable such phenomena remain.

A.1.5   Theory

We have proclaimed in the previous chapters that reality cannot be addressed without 'a theory' in mind. Theory shapes and directs our vision. In fact theory is the 'instrument' or carrier that allows us to see what we want to see and not always in the way we want to see it. Theory shapes and directs our vision. Implicitly, it means that we can articulate what is theoretical and what is worth being seen and, thus, emphasised. The relevant theory given a specific problem can be articulated in words. Just think for a moment about emotions, intuition or 'gut feeling'. Or think also about a popular construct such as 'emotional intelligence'. What we face here is a rational and often linear-causal approach to reality. Things can be identified, conceptualised in a logical construct and turned into measurable properties. Just imagine you would analyse the relationship with your partner in such a way and then present it to him or her. Do you think it would be a good idea? Not really.

A.1.6   Subjectivity

When designing research we make a selection (intuitively or consciously) out of an ongoing stream of events. The sheer fact of selecting certain events above others – the act of giving them additional attention – also called 'bracketing' (Weick 1979) puts an emphasis on them thus 'enlarging' them. Even if we respect the most stringent scholarliness bracketing remains something done by an actor based on his knowledge, experience and professionalism at the specific moment in time. Thus, it appears that by definition subjectivity in any research design is inescapable. If we accept this fundamental subjectivity of any research activity then justification becomes almost the only way to demonstrate the quality of a research design and subsequent process.

A.1.7   Ontology

We act in this world with limited knowledge. This largely accepted fact is also known as 'bounded rationality'. Not only is it simply impossible to know every-thing about everything, we can't even be sure we know what we know. What we know escapes our full understanding yet it is at the same time an unlimited source. This indirectly raises the issue of ontology: the overall conceptualisation of a field of knowledge not necessarily presented in a structured manner (see Glossary). In organisations we refer to this phenomenon as 'knowledge management'. Ontology in general relates to the assumptions we hold about reality – whether it is external or a construct of our mind. Knowledge can be attributed in part to be in the possession of people and at the same time a result of interactions. Since people cannot really define what they know in a specific field or regarding a particular topic it is only in interactions that they demonstrate and create knowledge. This complex phenome-non describes the social construction of knowledge. We recognise again here the two fundamental – positivist and constructivist – traditions, both of which are present in any research.

A.1.8   Epistemology

Epistemology can be described as the philosophy of knowledge, especially with regard to its methods, validity, nature, sources, limits and scope. It concerns the investigation of what distinguishes justified belief from opinion. "Lucky guesses or 'true' beliefs resulting from wishful thinking are not knowledge." (Craig 2005, p. 224). As such it is the 'quality assurance' of what we know. Still, specificity of what knowledge is remains a matter of controversy. "One view is that what distinguishes genuine knowledge from a lucky guess is justification; another is that the causation of the belief by facts verifies it." (Bullock and Trombley 1999). Justification is a central element to any research design and its outcome. The nature of the facts – i.e. the nature of the data and how they have been acquired – forms the cornerstone in such a design. We stick to the view that the logic of the argument used to select certain means (methods and techniques) for producing data and knowledge has to be reliable.

A.1.9   Deontology

If we explore critically the definition of methodology it shows a certain degree of 'mandatoriness': as a rule, what seems to be required is shared conviction. Despite the earlier stipulated emptiness of methodology we face an intriguing issue here called deontology. Deontology concerns the study of the nature of duty and obligation of 'what is necessary'. It is quite thought-provoking to consider the possible universe of methodologies for a moment as a collection of deontologies, each individual methodology specifying its own plan of action, the acts themselves and the consistent if not rational order in which actions have to be performed. The inevitable question is to what degree this deontological nature is free of normativity. Who decides on the appropriateness of the order of acts, their causality, their logic if not their appropriateness? We stumble upon a more philosophical discussion regarding the ontological nature of methodology. There is no need to elaborate any further here. Just be aware that any methodology is not 'natural' but driven by (historically) driven beliefs about acting. When finally defending your work this will be a key decisive factor – at least implicitly but almost certainly explicitly.

A.1.10   Finally: The Role of the Researcher

Given the reflections above it should be clear that conceptualising a problem is not only a craft it is also an art entailing the researcher to navigate between all kinds of theoretical, methodological, philosophical and other booby-traps and dilemmas. Any problem addressed in an organisation is a temporary valid construction of just a fraction of that specific reality. It is naïve and probably incorrect if the researcher is convinced he alone has the knowledge to clarify the nature and meaning of the problem at hand, be it at the start of the research or well underway. The researcher's most valid contribution is to conduct careful research into the nature, size, impact and meaning of a particular problem by means of various methodological approaches. Any research therefore should be conducted departing from – if not focusing on – the situation and people that 'create' the situation. If we recognise and accept the nature of the question this in itself is already a compass. To proceed in either a quantitative or qualitative way or a combination of both is elaborated in the following two chapters and Interlude II.

References

Bonjour, L. (1985). *The Structure of Empirical Knowledge*, Cambridge: Harvard University Press.

Blaikie, N. (1993). *Approaches to social enquiry*, Cambridge: Polity Press.

Bullock, A., Trombley, S. (1999). *The New Dictionary of Modern Thought*, London: HarperCollins.

Chisholm, R. (1989). *Theory of Knowledge*, Cambrige: Harvard University Press.

Craig, E. (eds.) (2005). *The Shorter Encyclopedia of Philosophy*, London: Routledge.

Griseri, P. (2002). *Management Knowledge: a critical view*, New York: Palgrave.

Johnson, P., Duberley, J. (2000). *Understanding management research: an introduction to epistemology*, London: Sage.n.

Chapter 4
Quantitative Research

Observing Through the Eyes of the Researcher Using a Closed Research Question

Abstract By means of the previously introduced Research Pyramid this chapter provides a concise overview of the quantitative research approach. The essence of quantitative research is to use a 'theory' to frame and thus understand the problem at hand. Its starting point if not focus can be to contribute to the development of theory. It is grounded in the basic attitude that knowledge about reality can also be obtained 'through the eyes of the researcher'. It is he who elaborates theory based on findings. In order to make this happen theory is most often translated into a conceptual model and elaborated predominantly by means of hypotheses. For the researcher conducting quantitative research implies carefully operationalising a theory and subsequently measuring it by means of variables and questions. He needs to justify the way in which he has designed and operationalised the research methodologically and technically.[1]

4.1 Introduction

Conducting research on the basis of a quantitative method or methodology has a long tradition. This tradition can be traced back historically to natural science. It is based on the postulation that knowledge about reality can only be obtained 'through the eyes of the researcher'. Quantitative roughly means in terms of 'quantities' implying the extent to which something either does or does not occur in terms of amount, number, frequency etc. A classical (quality) mantra such as 'to measure is to know' originates from this rich tradition. Anyone who conducts quantitative research, wants to know the degree to which something (a phenomenon, a specific kind of behaviour, such as the number of cups of coffee drunk during a day, the

---

[1]The tone of the current and following chapter is a bit matter-of-fact if not 'staccato'. The aim is to provide an overview of the essence of both methodological approaches, not to repeat what has been written already. Both chapters conclude by formulating some criticism towards the outlined approach.

J. Jonker and B. Pennink, *The Essence of Research Methodology*,
DOI 10.1007/978-3-540-71659-4_4, © Springer-Verlag Berlin Heidelberg 2010

duration of meeting in relation to the number of decisions etc.) occurs or not and if it does, to what degree. In other words quantitative research entails putting a theoretical construct to the test. The term 'quantity' also refers to measuring and counting. Typical questions for quantitative research are: How often does this occur? How many people use this service? How many complaints did we receive in the last quarter? Or: What do our customers perceive as our Unique Selling Points (USPs) and which of these is the most important to them? No wonder this approach contains a preference for working with numerical data, figures and statistics.

Quantitative research is initialised by means of a closed question that results in a problem definition appearing at the start of the research. The elaboration of the question is based on – a relevant amalgam of – existing theories. After this elaboration the problem is more or less definite and most of the time elaborated in a conceptual model.[2] The researcher carefully focuses on the methodological and technical 'translation' of the problem into research instruments (techniques) of which the most well know is the questionnaire followed by a structured and detailed interview guide. The way he goes about accomplishing this translation is almost fully determined in advance. The researcher departs from a fixed methodological approach that will offer him the 'technical' support needed. This will also enable him to be aware of the stage of the research at almost any time and what he is to do next. A set of stable and reliable requirements and criteria has been developed over time to assess the quality of a quantitative research. These criteria mainly aim at monitoring the way the researcher has designed and executed the research. The quantitative research approach is based upon an empirical cycle that has a deductive[3] nature.

Box 4.1: Examples of Closed Questions
(a) To what extent do visitors of our petrol station need an extension of our services?
(b) To what extent is the 'emotional neglect' in the organisation caused by the nature of our products?
(c) ...

4.2   The Box of Bricks: Closed Question

Quantitative research is based on a closed question. Once the question has been elaborated into a problem definition it will not change again during the course of research. Once some preliminary steps have been taken in the preparation of

---

[2]Please note that research based on a closed question can also start with an already existing model with a specific academic discipline. Based on this model often combined with the work of others new questions are formulated and tested.

[3]Deductive means: 'a method of reasoning where conclusions are deduced logically from other things that are already known' or '... a form of reasoning in which conclusions are formulated about particulars from general or universal premises.'

quantitative research it might be useful to apply the following checklist. This checklist addresses five key criteria that together define the quality of the problem definition.

Firstly: is it *researchable*? Is the subject accessible? Will people be willing to participate? One can dream of doing a project in which secret dreams about new markets of managers are being compared, but you might run into some problems here.

Secondly: is it *relevant*? What might be the possible outcome, the 'product' of the research and for whom has this outcome a specific value? Please always remember that what might be relevant for one stakeholder is not necessarily relevant for another! You need to define this relevance and communicate it.

Thirdly: is the project *informative*? Does the research generate new and fresh findings or does is just regenerate what we already know. You can write a perfect synopsis of existing literature – which is certainly not without value – but does it really tell us something new?

Fourthly: is it *reliable*? Is the work consistent and does it generate the same results when it is repeated? Consistency also helps us to know whether we can rely on the outcomes. Do they represent what really is the matter? Reliability is maybe the most important criterion in judging quantitative research.

Finally: is it *effective*? This effectiveness has two meanings. It can either apply to the way the research is being carried out, or it can apply to whether the research provides an effective answer to the original question. Assessing the effectiveness finally tells us something about the balance between means invested (time, money) and results obtained.

It is deemed handy to go through this checklist once some initial work has been done and solve any doubts before continuing. Once a clear definition of the problem is available, more detailed research is possible with the help of the conceptual model described in Chap. 3.

That model consists of:

- An outline of research elements; i.e., what does and what does not belong to the research
- A selection of characteristics (variables) of these elements
- A description of the nature of the relationships between the variables
- The formulation of hypotheses and suppositions based on the above (Fig. 4.1)

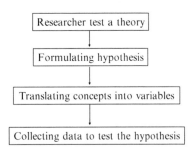

Fig. 4.1 Empirical cycle: deductive

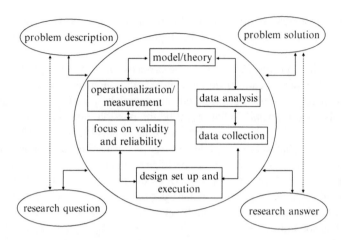

Fig. 4.2 The box of bricks: closed question

In quantitative research that is guided by a closed question, hypotheses play an important role. Hypotheses are expressed theoretical expectations that will be confronted with the empirical results gathered during the research activities. The research process can be described as an empirical cycle focused on deduction.

The basic outline concerns a theory being tested by the researcher, a theory elaborated in terms of hypotheses deducted from theory. Hypotheses are operationalised in terms of variables and questions that can be traced back directly to the theory. Finally, the researcher uses specific instruments to measure the variables. This general outline has been translated in the box of bricks guided by a closed question (Fig. 4.2).

A closed question elaborated with the help of the box of bricks provides a similar pattern. Actually hypotheses are not tested in all research pertaining from a closed question, but this approach is often used. Research activities focus on the problem description, solution, research question and research answer (objective). Furthermore it is necessary to check whether important preconditions (time, money, access etc.) that are required for the project, are fulfilled. The research activities consist of the search for theory and the formulation of a (conceptual) model. The notions used for a particular model need to be made operational and measurable. Subsequently, data are collected, for instance by means of questionnaires or highly structured interviews. These data will need to be analysed in the light of testing hypotheses. Obviously, each of the distinctive research activities can be assessed in terms of reliability and validity, as can the outcome.

> **Box 4.2: Relevance for Whom?**
> The general question about relevance is an important one. This becomes clear if we also consider with whom and in which way discussions about relevance have taken place. Was there a real dialogue or was one powerful stakeholder imposing his view of relevance? This doesn't mean that it is always necessary to have a dialogue in every case. Yet in every project the question whether it is necessary to have a dialogue should be addressed. Besides investigating practical implications always the issue of theoretical relevance must be raised.

> **Box 4.3: Checklist of a Problem Definition**
>
> | | Yes | Doubt | No |
> | --- | --- | --- | --- |
> | Researchable | ( ) | ( ) | ( ) |
> | Relevance | ( ) | ( ) | ( ) |
> | Informative | ( ) | ( ) | ( ) |
> | Reliable | ( ) | ( ) | ( ) |
> | Effectiveness | ( ) | ( ) | ( ) |
>
> Fill in and check. In case of doubts please go back to your research design, improve and check again.

> **Box 4.4: Start of Quantitative Research**
>
> | | Yes | No |
> | --- | --- | --- |
> | Problem 'image' | ( ) | ( ) |
> | Research question | ( ) | ( ) |
> | Research objective | ( ) | ( ) |
> | Preconditions | ( ) | ( ) |
>
> When all four questions can be answered with 'yes', the research can start! This might mean building a conceptual model.

4.3 Quantitative Paradigm

Quantitative research is based on the basic approach that knowledge about reality can be obtained 'through the eyes of the researcher'. It is common to call this the expert approach. It is the researcher who – from behind his desk – creates an image of the phenomenon to be examined. This is done by means of a careful and consistent study of literature, accepted concepts and current findings by others, which are then used to help formulate the problem definition, research objective and research question. This approach can be expressed in several *fundamentals:*

- At the start of the research it is the researcher that formulates a theory about the reality he is going to examine
- The researcher is an 'expert' regarding the subject as well as its content
- The researcher conducts research in 'the' reality (the empirical situation to be examined) by means of carefully chosen instruments
- The chosen – respectively especially developed – instruments form the primary source for numerical data
- The researcher observes 'through his own eyes', in other words, by designing and realising the research he determines what is observed or measured – and what is left out
- The researcher attempts to test the theoretical constructs as represented by the model he has developed
- The researcher pays great attention to methods and techniques; this care determines to a great extent the quality of the research

The attitude of the quantitative researcher, as described above, implies that he tries to be an objective (or: neutral) observer. He is not personally involved in the phenomena that are being examined and will strive to be as objective and independent as possible in the research at all times. It is crucial to carefully justify 'how and why' he has examined the question in the way he has, why he has chosen the underlying theory, how it relates to the developed variables and so forth. The choices will need to be made in such a way that if any other researcher repeats the research, he will make similar choices. When applying these fundamentals to drawing up a *research design* it will show that the researcher:

- Preferably operates on the basis of a closed and relatively structured research design that precisely matches the subject being examined
- Carefully and deliberately develops theory and related concepts as soon as possible
- Uses an empirical cycle that is deductive by nature
- Utilises a small spectrum of deliberately generated (numerical) data sources, of which the most important ones originate from surveys
- Opts for structured data collections within a precisely determined sample in a clearly outlined target population
- Systematically classifies and analyses the generated data, for example using the computer (SPSS)
- Eventually allocates meaning to the research results on the basis of analyses and subsequently translates them for the client

The implication of these fundamentals for the *course of research* is that:

- Activities are based on a fixed methodology that, with small exceptions, is determined in advance

- Existing theory and theoretical insights are collected and processed at the beginning as they form the future basis for the elaboration of the research
- Phases – or steps – in the research are consecutive and mostly linear
- The researcher needs the results of previous steps in his research in order to outline the next step
- The questions of a survey are linked to variables, which are linked to a conceptual model that is directly deduced from theory
- In order to justify his elaboration of the research in terms of measuring instruments, the researcher will constantly focus on consistency between the various steps
- The researcher initially operates by means of a set of data he has generated with his instruments
- The set of data represents 'the reality' and consists of 'objective facts'
- A sharp distinction can be made between the facts the researcher is working with and the way he interprets them
- Any other researcher who conducts the same research will principally generate similar facts and results

The outcome of quantitative research is the testing of a theory or theoretical insights in a predetermined reality. Depending on the points of departure used the research can be repeated in a different situation using a combination of quantitative and qualitative methods and techniques. Contradictory results can indicate questions for future research. It might also be possible to develop some 'sensitising concepts' (see Chap. 5) that may provide the start of pure qualitative research. In this respect, qualitative and quantitative research can be put to use in a complementary way (also see Interlude II).

Box 4.5: The Flow of Quantitative Research
1. Start: unprocessed problem
2. Problem definition, research objective and research question
3. Search for relevant theory
4. Development of a conceptual model
5. Creation of a research design
6. Data collection and data processing
7. Interpretation
8. Reporting

4.4 Quantitative Methodology

In quantitative methodologies a distinction is often made between research aimed at testing hypotheses afterwards (ex post facto research) versus research conducted experimentally. The most important distinction between both approaches is the degree to which the researcher is able to intervene in the research field. In *ex post facto* research the researcher is *not* able to intervene, whereas in experimental research the researcher *can* intervene. Pure experiments comprise a control group, an experimental group and a random classification of those involved with the research. Both groups then need to be compared before (zero measurement) and after a treatment (post measurement). This is hardly feasible in business situations. *Ex post facto* research is widespread. Most research in a business situation is characterised as a case study. This means nothing more than observing during or after certain events s; the researcher is not able to intervene intentionally and to determine the possible effect of that intervention. In order to be able to make predictions about possible effects the researcher will need to compare his results. This remains a complicated and often biased affair. The researcher can choose between the possibilities such as a norm or another existing case or a theory. When the researcher has made his choice (on solid grounds) he will consolidate his research activities into specific quantitative methods.

4.5   Quantitative Methods and Techniques

It is impossible to provide a brief overview of quantitative methods; the literature in this area is too abundant (see Jupp 2006). Therefore, the examples below should be viewed as a small selection intended simply to illustrate the range of what is available.

Firstly, let us look at the approach described by Tacq (1997). This approach involves an analysis of the research question to establish relevant concepts and how they are related to one another. Let's say that the research question contains two concepts and a simple relationship connecting them. For example the concepts could be 'the level of the reward' and 'the satisfaction of employees' and the relationship: the higher the reward the more satisfaction. When the constructs are operationalised (see Chap. 3) into variables the measurement level has to be decided. It then becomes appropriate to decide which statistical technique could be used. In essence this approach is looking for underlying concepts and their connections. It then compares these with the predetermined relations in specific statistical techniques. A multiple regression analysis for example includes complex relations between the variables that have to fit with the suggested hypothesis within the research question. This specific technique stresses the importance of looking for a logical connection between the research question and statistical models. (see also Box 4.6)

However, this specific technique requires the researcher to collect a substantial amount of data from a large number of employees in the organisation.

A second more simplified example concerns the construction of an 'analytical plan'. This means that a researcher constructs a plan in which he describes in what way and with what kind of statistical techniques and computer models the data will be analysed.

In the context of quantitative research it is also possible to point at the use of case studies in a specific way. As a third example here, Yin (2003) points out the necessity to choose a so-called 'critical case'. The researcher selects such a case to find out if it meets certain (pre-formulated) expectations that are derived from an existing theory. If these expectations are not met, then the theory will be rejected. The researcher should try to select his case as critically as possible.

These three examples concern analytical methods. In general, the data collection process is highly structured. Questionnaires are pre-coded, observations are structured and interviews are standardized. This way a lot of data will be comparable. The most frequently used method to generate data is the questionnaire, followed by the collection of existing data material from the organisation (e.g., annual reports, financial reports and so forth). In a limited number of cases observations are also used – but often as an addition to the mainstream research (see Triangulation).

Box 4.6: Examples of Statistical Techniques

It is beyond the scope of this book to treat the statistical techniques but to name some really good publications we start with Siegel's "Non parametric statistics" (1956). It is a book that goes into detail with respect to the possible relations between variables on low level of measurement. If the variables are at least on the interval level then an excellent book will be Horton's "The general linear model" (1978). And if the dependent variable is on a low measurement level and the independent on at least interval, then Winer's "Statistical principles in experimental design" (1971) is a good choice. See also the references at the end of this chapter.

4.6 Quantitative Research Criticised

The previous section indicates that the quantitative research method has a long and rich tradition that is also supported by a wide choice of methodological, methodical and instrumental possibilities. Conducting research in this way provides the researcher with an approach that adheres to the academic, respectively scientific tradition and will therefore be widely recognised. Since the final research justification (see Chaps. 6 and 8) often takes place in front of a so-called 'academic forum' that is familiar with this approach, the researcher can be fairly sure – provided that he has worked accurately – that the research is 'sound'. Nevertheless, it cannot be denied that this approach also has potential weaknesses. Important points of criticism are that the researcher:

- Works on the basic assumption that 'theory' can represent the reality of the problem as it occurs within a certain context
- Examines a 'reality' that is detached from the one in which 'real' people live
- Meticulously adheres to a strict methodical approach that does not leave any margin for unexpected developments in the field
- Works with a conceptual model that is methodically and technically sound, but does not provide information about the actual phenomenon

- Pays excessive attention to the technical details of the research and in particular to measuring techniques and – procedures
- Shows excessive respect to figures – that are generated intentionally – perceived as objective facts
- Has only apparent – or instrumental – neutrality
- Always implies to interpret the generated data before they become meaningful again – figures do not speak for themselves
- Has to have his results translated by the organisation involved in order to make them relevant if not applicable

4.7   Chapter Summary

This chapter has briefly described the quantitative research approach by means of the underpinning paradigm, methodology, method and techniques.

- The essence of quantitative research is that the researcher tests theory by means of a conceptual model.
- Quantitative research has a clear starting and finishing point.
- The quantitative researcher is as objective as possible regarding the research that needs to be conducted in order to strive for maximal objectivity.
- Quantitative research is based on a strict methodical approach through which it is possible to determine whether the researcher has operated accurately.
- In this type of research predominantly numerical data are used.
- The systematic analysis of data is done using statistical methods that are supported by computer programmes (SPSS in particular).
- Interpreting the results of quantitative research generally occurs on the basis of the researcher's interpretation.
- The translation of research results into application possibilities is the 'underdog' of this kind of research.

References

Allen, M. J. & Yen, W. M. (2001). *Introduction to measurement theory*. Pacific Groove: Brooks Cole.
Bollen, K. A. (1989). *Structural equations with latent variables*. New York: Wiley.
Box, G. E. P., Hunter, J. S., & Hunter, W. G. (2005). *Statistics for experimenters*. New Jersey: Wiley.
Buckingham, A. & Saunders, P. (2004). *The survey methods handbook*. Cambridge: Polity Press.
Crano, W. D. & Brewer, M. B. (2002). *Principles and methods of social research*. New Jersey: Lawrence Erlbaum Associates Publishers.
Dewberry, C. (2004). *Statistical methods for organizational research: theory and practice*. London: Routledge.
Dul, J. & Hak, T. (2007). *Case study methodology in business research*. Oxford (UK): Butterworth-Heinemann/Elsevier Science.

Hair, J. F., Black, W. C., Babin, B. J., Anderson, R. E., & Tatham, R. L. (2006). *Multivariate data analysis*. New Jersey: Prentice Hall.

Ho, R. (2006). *Handbook of univariate and multivariate data analysis and interpretation with SPSS*. Florida: Chapman and Hall.

Horton, R. L. (1978). *The general linear model: data analysis in the social and behavioral sciences*. London: McGraw-Hill.

Johnson, R. A. & Wichern, D. W. (2002). *Applied multivariate statistical analysis* (5th ed.). Upper Saddl: Tice Hall.

Jupp, V. (ed). (2006). *The sage dictionary of social research methods*. London: Sage.

Keller, G. (2005). *Statistics for management and economics*. California: Thomson Brooks.

Morrison, D. F. (2005). *Multivariate statistical methods*. California: Thomson Brooks.

Siegel, S. (1956). *Nonparametric statistics for the behavioral sciences*. New York: McGraw-Hill.

Tacq, J. J. A. (1997). *Multivariate analysis in social sciences research*. London: Sage.

Winer, B. J. C. (1962). *Statistical principles in experimental design*. Tokyo: McGraw-Hill.

Yin, R. K. (2003). *Case study research*. Beverly Hills: Sage.

Chapter 5
Qualitative Research

Observing Through the Eyes of Someone Else
Using an Open Research Question

Abstract The essence of qualitative research is to identify the characteristics and structure of phenomena and events examined in their natural context. Subsequently, these characteristics are brought together to form a mini theory or a conceptual model. Conducting qualitative research requires an 'open' attitude in order to understand how others experience their situation. As in the previous chapter, this chapter provides a concise overview of qualitative methodology, methods and techniques. The demonstration of the various methods is done on the basis of 'grounded theory', in accordance with the chain reasoning of Toulmin and action research. This chapter finishes again with some critical analysis and a summary.

5.1 Introduction

The term 'quality' in this context refers to the way in which knowledge can be developed, the corresponding attitude and behaviour of the researcher, as well as the chosen methodology and kind of data. It is research in which the researcher makes an attempt to understand a specific organisational reality and occurring phenomena from the perspective of those involved. He tries to grasp it 'from the inside out' contrarily to 'from the outside in' – which was fundamental to quantitative methodology. The researcher does not start his research by means of theoretical notions, or a model or concepts that needs to be tested, but with several sensitising concepts. Sensitising concepts are pre-theoretical by nature and serve to steer observations. Implicitly, this supposes that theoretical knowledge about a specific phenomenon is incomplete, insufficient or ineffective at the start of a research project. The researcher's basic attitude needs to be as unprejudiced as possible (some say even: as blank as a white sheet of paper) in an attempt to achieve full and almost 'pure' understanding of people's behaviour in certain situations. The essence is: 'a systematic search for the unknown'. In order to achieve this, the researcher will try to become one with the situation that is being examined. During the research, he will respect the situation of those involved as much as possible, not

J. Jonker and B. Pennink, *The Essence of Research Methodology*,
DOI 10.1007/978-3-540-71659-4_5, © Springer-Verlag Berlin Heidelberg 2010

only by observing the working situation, but also by partaking in other activities such as chatting at the coffee machine or having lunch in the canteen, so that he becomes fully integrated into the organisation. In this approach research is a continuous process. For example, the messages on the notice board in a company may provide valuable data, or the amount of graffiti in the car park or the table order during specific meetings. In order to steer his research activities and justify the results, a researcher may opt for either a certain methodology or combination of methodologies (so-called 'multi-method approach' – see the next Interlude). The objective of qualitative research is to search for – and develop – a theory or as one author writes, "... should be theoretically driven rather than deformed by technical considerations (What can be measured? What can be sampled?)". These theoretical notions may possibly lead to a 'mini-theory'. A mini-theory is a theory that is applicable for one particular situation. It still needs to prove its general validity. By repeating the research the mini-theory may develop into a theory that is useful in various situations and at particular times: a 'grand theory' (see Strauss and Corbin 1990). Once theoretical insights have been developed, they will need to be understood by, and be useful to, those involved. In many cases this implies that the people examined participate in the research in one way or another.

5.2   The Box of Bricks: Open Question

Qualitative research is characterised by the fact that the researcher works on the basis of an open question.

In the course of research this question can (and will) change. It may take a while before the exact interpretation of the formulated question, its boundaries and meaning becomes clear. The process in which the question obtains its definite shape occurs on the basis of an empirical cycle which is inductive by nature and always relates to the world of those involved (Fig. 5.1).

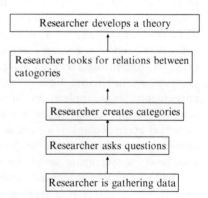

Fig. 5.1 Empirical cycle:
Inductive

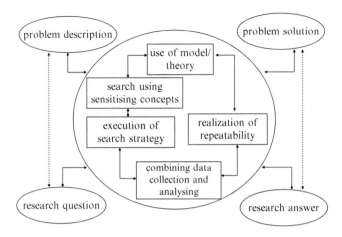

Fig. 5.2 The box of bricks: open question

Contrary to the empirical cycle in the previous chapter, which results in the confirmation or rejection of a theory, the inductive cycle results in new theory or elements that could lead to a theory. Statements are deduced from all kinds of data with the objective of obtaining theoretical insights. These insights may be tested in a next empirical cycle, this time deductively instead of inductively (Fig. 5.2).

The box of bricks can be designed with an open question in mind. Once again, the problem description, research questions, research answers and possible solutions form the core of research activities. The activities based on an open question differ from those for a box of bricks with a closed question. In order to make both boxes comparable, the theory (and) (or) model represent a key component. Yet, combined with the sensitising concepts, theory only plays a different and often modest role. It is a starting point, but no more than that. The systematic search for new insights is central to the research activities. Data collection and analysis will take place simultaneously. In the evaluation of a inductive research project transparency and comprehensiveness are important. Reliability in such a project will be hardly subject for discussion. What is more important here is whether those involved and being investigated are allowed and able to give meaning to the findings.

Box 5.1: Examples of Open Questions
(a) What do people do when they communicate with each other?
(b) Why is it that our meetings always take place in a disorderly fashion?
(c) How do we shape our relationships with our suppliers?
(d) How come there has been such a 'grumpy' atmosphere lately?
(e) What is the key issue in our managerial decision processes?

5.3   Qualitative Paradigm

Qualitative research is based on the fact that knowledge about reality can only be obtained through 'the eyes of someone else'. It is common to call this the 'actor approach'. This basic attitude is expressed in several *fundamentals:*

- Developing a theory about the reality of a particular situation without interactions about this theory with the people who are part of the investigated reality is something the researcher will try to avoid as much as possible
- The researcher is not an expert but an 'explorer' – he hopes to find
- The researcher does not conduct the research in a specific 'reality' (empirical situation), but 'within' a specific context
- This context is the primary data source
- The researcher will try to 'look through the eyes of someone else' or at least make a systematic attempt to understand and respect the actors perspective
- The researcher will try to develop insight into and understanding of actions and meanings within a certain social context while paying attention to time and process
- The researcher will act with respect for the phenomenon that he is examining, based on the assumption that the people involved attach meaning to the phenomenon

This basic approach implies that the researcher cannot be an objective outsider. As a person, the researcher is involved with both his own research and the phenomena that are being examined. At the same time, he will need to justify how he conducted the research, why he chose this particular approach, how the research process took place and what the reasons were for his choices in carrying out the project. In such a situation, operating and making choices cannot be done without direct personal involvement. These fundamentals have the following implications for the research *design*. They mean

- Working with relatively open and unstructured research designs that connect to the examined phenomenon
- The use of the inductive cycle rather than the deductive cycle
- Utilising a broad spectrum of possible data sources of which the most important ones are observation, informal conversation and in-depth interviews
- A preference for unstructured data collection
- Avoiding the use of theory and concepts during the early stages of research
- Data should be collected and analysed systematically, yet quantification plays a minor role

As regards the course of research these fundamentals imply that:

- Existing theoretical insights can be used at different moments in time or in different ways during the research
- Different phases of research influence and interact with each other – they are often cyclic rather than linear

- In order to be able to provide the reasons for his different considerations and choices afterwards, the researcher will use a journal or diary
- The researcher will search (repeatedly) through different data sources (triangulation principle[1]), until the data collection is complete (so-called saturation)
- It is difficult to make a clear distinction between objective facts and individual interpretations. In order to avoid this difficult distinction the researcher could make use of the distinction between first order data: the so-called objective data such as sales figures or other figures; second order data: information from the people involved and, finally, third order data: the use of his own information. This distinction into sorts of data appears in the appendix of one of Morgan's most well-known books (1993)
- It is often difficult to make a clear-cut distinction between interpretations by the researcher or by the people involved

The result of qualitative research – the development of a mini theory with local validity – can form the basis for a subsequent qualitative (and) (or) quantitative research. The research can be repeated using the same methods and techniques in different situations. It is also possible to test the developed mini-theory by means of quantitative methods. In this way, qualitative and quantitative research are complementary and not opposites (see Interlude II).

Box 5.2: The Flow of Qualitative Research
1. Start: 'unprocessed' and 'open' problem
2. Instrument(s) for data collection (various sources)
3. Transcription of data
4. First classification of data
5. Narrowing down the analysis
6. Further analysis (possibly with new data)
7. Reporting and writing

   Adapted from Wester et al. (2000)

5.4 Qualitative Methodology

Different methodologies are distinguishable in the qualitative research approach. A common classification is according to ethnography, ethnomethodology and phenomenology. It is also possible to make a classification on the basis of the extent to which the researcher does or does not participate in daily affairs: the so-called 'non-participating observation strategies' or the 'participating observation strategies'.

---

[1]The triangulation principle concerns the use of different techniques and methods in the same study to collect data so as to verify the validity of any findings enhancing their robustness. Triangulation can take place on different *levels* and have different *meanings* depending on the paradigmatic choice. We expand on the latter in Interlude II.

Regardless of the classification chosen, it remains difficult to distinguish sharply between the different methodologies. An important point is the fact that different methodologies have been developed for different contexts with various scientific purposes in mind. As a result, a specific methodology has its own framework of assumptions, professional language, approach and rules. The researcher is free – depending on the question, sensitising concepts and context – to choose an appropriate methodology for his qualitative research. Still, when examined more closely, it appears that different methodologies have more in common than was originally thought. In Miles and Hubermans' 'tree' diagram this becomes clearly visible (see Fig. 5.3).

Careful studying and consideration of available methodologies is necessary in order to avoid getting confused when making a choice for the research design. Therefore, the following criteria should be taken into account:

- The nature of the phenomenon to be examined
- The research direction indicated by the question
- Possible existing 'sensitising concepts'
- The nature of the data
- The researcher's personal preference

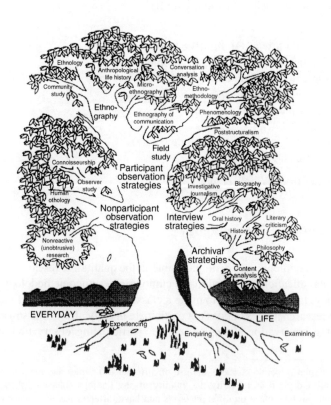

Fig. 5.3 Qualitative research strategies. Miles and Huberman (1994)

It can also be the case that – after thorough consideration – the researcher starts using a specific methodology and then gradually refines it. This may imply that observing in a certain situation marks the start of the research. The results of these observations may for instance lead to a refinement into ethno-methodology that makes it possible to focus on analysing communication patterns. Regardless which methodology is chosen, it is important to take into account that the search behaviour does not conflict with the fundamentals that have been formulated in advance. When this is the case, the researcher should report and elaborate it. After all, it may be possible these moments lead to new insights.

Yin (2003) has also to be referred to here. In the context of qualitative research Yin has made an important contribution to qualitative methodology by focusing on case-study design. Case study research is in his terms: 'Using a limited number of units of analysis within their natural conditions. In choosing the cases the researcher should use arguments that are related to the topic under research. There should be enough diversity and richness in the sampling to allow for the construction of theory. This is generally called 'theoretical sampling'. In studying the cases a researcher should take into consideration whether he studies each case as a whole or if he only studies certain aspects of the case. Here there is a clear relation with the systems-theoretical concept of embeddedness and the zooming in and out effect (see Chap. 3). Yin uses a cross-tabulation of two dimensions: studying one case versus a few cases and studying on the level of the whole versus studying specific aspects of a particular case.

> **Box 5.3: The Focus of a Case Study**
> Use the two dimensions described in the text to construct the suggested cross-tabulation. Imagine how you would fill in the cells in your own research.

5.5 Qualitative Methods

Although initially the distinction between methodology and method seems to be clear, when qualitative research is put into practice this may not to be the case. What is more, these terms are often used with the term instrument in one and the same breath, which can cause confusion. For instance, what one author may call methodology seems, when examined more closely, to be a method (e.g. see Strauss and Corbin 1990). It also appears that a methodology only provides global instructions, while it hardly deserves to be called 'a method'. Nevertheless, it is useful to maintain the distinction between both terms for as long and as consistently as possible so that the researcher is able to justify his actions. During the course of his work, the researcher will give his own interpretation to the use of a specific method and develop a clear preference for it. Nonetheless, anyone who is careless in the use of these methods may end up 'messing around' and, thus, wasting time leading to improper results. Three examples of qualitative methods are outlined below. These are: the grounded theory approach (GT), the chain reasoning

approach, according to Toulmin, and action research. Each example will be
described briefly.

5.5.1 Example 1: Grounded Theory (GT)

The primary goal of GT is the development of a theory that is 'grounded' in
practice. Theory is developed during data collecting and subsequently coding the
material. The data material is used to search for categories, characteristics of these
categories and relationships between them. This is based on the principle of
'continuous comparison'. Various authors have developed different phases. Wester
(1987) recommends the following phases:

1. Exploration: to identify terms
2. Specification: to develop terms
3. Reduction: to determine the central term
4. Integration: to elaborate the theory

Central to grounded theory is the development of a theory that is grounded in the
'local' reality of the situation that will be investigated. With the help of the
sensitising concepts (see Chap. 3) at the start and the method of continuous
comparison, the researcher tries to develop the sensitising concepts into concepts
filled with elements that are emerging from the data (in this sense the *grounding*
develops). In practice the researcher starts with open coding. In this phase the
researcher develops categories appearing in the material. He then tries to find more
'proof' in the material to further support that category or to refine others. In the
second phase after finishing the refinement of the categories, the researcher tries to
find relations between the categories. This is what Strauss and Corbin (1990) call
the *axial coding process*.

    In the different phases of coding the researcher should keep the idea in mind that
he systematically writes down and uses his own reflections and considerations in
the research process as a source of data. On the whole, the researcher should keep in
mind the following points:

5.5.2 The GT Instructions

- Keep a diary and note down all relevant activities from the start
- Work on the basis of memos (theoretical notions in development)
- Constantly compare and integrate
- Apply plural data sources (triangulation)
- Use the existing theory of notions at different moments during the research
- Continue until the point of saturation has been reached. It is difficult to indicate
  this point but you know that you have reached it when new findings do not
  produce any new insights

5.5.3   Example 2: Chain Reasoning According to Toulmin

Toulmin et al. (1979) has developed a method that results in the construction of 'chain reasoning'. The chain's value resides in making arguments and conclusions explicit. It makes clear which data and claims were used for the line of reasoning. The results make it possible to ask clarifying questions.

The method of chain reasoning consists of three steps:

- Composing a first 'triad' (basic reasoning); this takes place on the basis of claims, grounds and warrants
- The second step is the introduction of support (using backing)
- The third step is the involvement of probabilities in the reasoning using 'rebuttals' and 'modal qualifiers' in the terms of Toulmin

5.5.4   The Instructions of Chain Reasoning

In order to compose a correct chain of reasoning, six elements can be used, which are:

- Claim
- Data or grounds
- Warrants
- Backing
- Rebuttals or reservations
- Modal qualifier

With the help of this basic order the researcher can construct a clear view of the arguments that can be deduced from the analysed text and the way they can be arranged. For a fuller description of how this works, please refer to Bromley (1986) (Fig. 5.4).

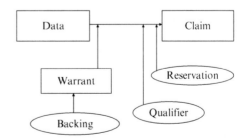

Fig. 5.4 Chain reasoning: data versus claim. Toulmin et al. (1979)

5.5.5   Example 3: Action Research

The researcher develops insight into an organisational 'reality' by cooperating in that reality and, where necessary or relevant, sympathising with those involved. By participating in the world of the people involved and supporting the introduction of changes, the researcher will be able to develop his own observations of the problem along the way. In this respect, the essence of the methodology is sharing and exchanging views and ideas during the task at hand, while at the same time reporting and registering everything that happens (also see Whitehead and Mcniff 2006).

5.5.6   Guidelines for Action Research

Guidelines for action research are aimed predominantly at the researcher's attitude. He will need to adopt an attitude similar to someone who is directly involved. Moreover, he will need to take sides and describe reality from within that position. It goes without saying that action research bares the danger of strong subjectivity. Creating the change becomes the primary target instead of developing a thorough understanding of a specific situation. If you notice that your research project is turning into a form of action research please register why and when this is happening and discuss it with you supervisor and the people involved. Some people consider action research as no research at all!

The three different methods[2] examples have been chosen deliberately in order to show the extensive range and content of qualitative methods. During a qualitative research project different methods can – if expedient – be used together or consecutively. This requires careful consideration and justification by the researcher:

- With regard to the objectives that need to be achieved
- With regard to the (theoretical) values that different methods are presumed to produce
- Taking practical aspects into account (time and energy)
- When combining the (results of) different methods
- The review of a specific research design as a whole (justification)

In addition to the above the researcher should also take the choice and application of (qualitative) techniques into account.

---

[2]Please realise that 'methods' and 'methodologies' are one and the same in this context. This observation leads to a rather fundamental debate that you might stumble upon when writing your Master Thesis or PhD. Please be aware!

5.6   Qualitative Techniques

Predominantly linguistic data will be used in a qualitative research approach. Conversation (in different forms) is the most frequent 'instrument' to generate data, followed by observations by the researcher. These instruments can be considered as a form of visual data. Usually, this involves conversations (whether or not deliberately held) being recorded. The results are then classified and analysed.

Classification implies that the researcher indicates how he will divide the available material into usable 'pieces' or 'chunks'. For instance, conversations can be cut into sentences, in turns or into 'mini paragraphs'. Whatever the chosen units of data are, they should always contain a meaning either brought to them by the researcher or by the respondents.

It is also possible to choose to classify consecutively all statements – respectively sentences – of one respondent. The choice for a certain classification strongly depends on the form of analysis chosen. Is the researcher concerned about discovering notions and categories? Is his attention focused on the way people communicate with each other during a conversation? Does the problem revolve around the interaction patterns during group meetings? Each of these choices forces a particular classification. Please note that there are many electronic aids that have been developed to facilitate the classification and analysis of these kinds of data. However, these will not be discussed here.

> **Box 5.4: Classifying Conversations**
> You have a conversation with three different people in an organisation. In your view each person makes a valuable contribution to the research. How will you justify this opinion? How will you clarify this? How are going to show this?

Box 5.5: Analysing a Simple Conversation (1)
Examine the text below; it concerns a transcription of a conversation within an organisation.
　　She says, "I cannot work with this program".
　　He says, "What is the matter?"
　　She says, "I cannot cope".
　　He says, "You said you would ask a professional?"
　　She says, "He says he can't look at it for a while".
　　He says, "Shall I have a look at it?"
　　She says, "Please, if you would".
　　He says, "All right, I will have a quick look".
Research questions:
With the above text in mind, try answering the following questions:

1. What is the matter in this situation? What is the matter here? What's the problem? Does everybody share the same opinion?
2. How could you gain insight into what exactly is happening? What kind of approach would you use to obtain this insight? Please try to be explicit.

Box 5.6: Interview Processing
In order to collect the data you need, you decide to conduct five interviews. Apart from the question as to how you will carry out these interviews, it also important to establish how you will process them. What are you going to do with the data afterwards (condensed summary, full transcription, etc.)? How are you going to draw up the reports? Which techniques will you use? Have you considered asking for feedback from the interviewees once you have done the processing? This opens up all kind of questions that can be helpful.

5.7　Qualitative Research Criticised

From the above, it becomes obvious that the qualitative research approach comprises a rich range of methodological, methodical and instrumental possibilities. Conducting such research makes it easier to relate the approach to the phenomena in the organisation. This approach is also open to some criticism. The most important criticism is:

- The frayed outline of the initial research question; working with an open question means working with uncertainty
- An often poor distinction between diagnosis, design and change

- The lack of an explicit theoretical framework, concept or model at the start of the research
- The often problematic relationship with a classical research design, whether or not in the form of a case study
- The character of qualitative data – 'difficult to revise' – and the great variety of data alternatives
- The explicit acknowledgement of the researcher's subjectivity; he is not an outsider but someone who is involved
- The poor distinction between methodologies and methods and the fact that similar instruments are applicable
- The poor distinction between facts and interpretations
- The 'open end' character of the course of research
- The low repeatability of a research approach that has only been conducted once
- The impossibility to precisely describe results in advance
- The low applicability of 'classical' methodological criteria in order to assess results

This criticism is only valid if the qualitative research approach is assessed solely on the basis of those standards that are applicable in well-conducted qualitative research (see Chap. 5). Nevertheless, it would be advisable to assess a specific type of (business) research – either quantitative or qualitative – primarily with regard to criteria which have been developed specifically for this intention. Research designs, in which inspiration has been gained from both angles, require highly precise reasoning to justify the assessment and criteria used. Yet, this is more of a challenge than a problem (see Interlude II).

5.7.1   Box 5.7: Analysing a Simple Conversation (2)

Look back at box 5.6 and take a closer look at the conversation. What would happen if the researcher knew what the 'he' thinks and what the 'she' thinks or what both feel? And what consequences could this have for the analyses.

5.8   Chapter Summary

This chapter has briefly described the qualitative research approach, outlining the paradigm, methodology, method and techniques.

- The essence of qualitative research is the researcher who tries to understand (and to explain) how people experience their (work) situation.
- Qualitative research is aimed at discovering characteristics in a particular situation and is initiated by an open question.
- Each qualitative research project will have to justify the role of those involved in the research activities.

- The qualitative researcher is completely involved in his research; this can easily result in uncontrollable subjectivity.
- Qualitative research offers the researcher the freedom to contribute his own interpretation to the methodological elaboration of his research.
- The most important source of data is linguistic (conversations, interview, etc.) combined with observations and memo's.
- The systematic analysis (transcription, classification, coding and interpretation) is generally given little attention in this type of research.
- Given the open character, it is often difficult to indicate the starting and finishing point; the researcher does not know when the research is finished.
- The qualitative research approach is particularly useful in conducting research within organisations.
- The results of qualitative research can be tested by means of a quantitative research approach; in this way both are complementary instead of contradictory.

References

Bromley, D. B. (1986). *The case study in psychology and related discipline*. Chichester: Wiley.
Coghlan, D. & Brannick, T. (2005). *Doing action research in your own organization*. London: Sage.
Creswell, J. (2008). *Qualitative inquiry and research design*. London: Sage.
David, M. (ed). (2006). *Case study research*. London: Sage.
Dul, J. & Hak, T. (2007). *Case study methodology in business research*. Oxford: Butterworth-Heinemann.
Flick, U. (2006). *An introduction to qualitative research* (3rd ed.). London: Sage.
Gummesson, E. (1999). *Qualitative methods in management research*. London: Sage.
Jupp, V. (ed). (2006). *The Sage dictionary of social research methods*. London: Sage.
Lawrence George, A. & Bennett, A. (2005). *Case studies and theory development in the social sciences*. Cambridge: MIT.
Mason, J. (2005). *Qualitative researching*. London: Sage.
Maxwell, J. A. (2005). *Qualitative research design: an interactive approach*. Thousand Oaks, CA: Sage.
McNeill, P. & Chapman, S. (2005). *Research methods*. London: Routledge.
Miles, M. B. & Huberman, A. M. (1994). *An expanded sourcebook. Qualitative data analysis*. London: Sage.
Millar, G. & Dingwall, R. (eds). (1997). *Context and method in qualitative research*. London: Sage.
Morgan. (1993). *Imaginization, the art of creative management*. Newbury Park, CA: Sage.
Moustakas, C. (1990). *Heuristic research, design; methodology and application*. London: Sage.
Schön, D. A. (1983). *The reflective practitioner*. New York: Basic Books.
Stake, R. E. (1995). *The art of case study research*. London: Sage.
Stanczak, G. (2006). *Visual research methods*. London: Sage.
Strauss, A. L. & Corbin, J. (1990). *Basics of qualitative research; grounded theory procedures and techniques*. London: Sage.
Toulmin, S., Rieke, R., & Janik, A. (1979). *An introduction to reasoning*. New York: Macmillan.
van Maanen, J. (1983). *Qualitative methodology*. Newbury Park, CA: Sage.
Wester, F. (1987). *Strategieën voor Kwalitatief Onderzoek*. Muiderberg: Coutinho.

Wester, F., Smaling, A., & Mulder, L. (2000). *Praktijkgericht Kwalitatief Onderzoek*. Bussum: Coutinho.
Whitehead, J. & McNiff, J. (2006). *Action research: living theory*. London: Sage.
Willis, J. (2007). *Foundations of qualitative research: interpretive and critical approaches*. London: Sage.
Yin, R. K. (2003). *Case study research: design and methods*. Thousand Oaks, CA: Sage.

Interlude II Combining a Qualitative and Quantitative Approach in One Research Design

Qualitative Researcher

"Many people these days are bored with their work and are . . ."

Quantitative Researcher (Interrupting)

"Which people? How many of them? When do they feel this way? Where do they work? What do they do? Why are they bored? How long have they felt this way? What are their needs? When do they feel excited? Where did they come from? What parts of their work bother them most? Which . . .?"

Qualitative Researcher

"Never mind".[3]

A.1 Combining a Qualitative and Quantitative Approach in One Research Design

This second interlude advocates the combined use of a qualitative and quantitative approach. The key success factor is an alternating step-wise use of quantitative and qualitative approaches throughout the process of your research. Three different phases which permit the use of different approaches are distinguished. In each phase the chosen methodology should be supported by relevant methods and

---

[3]This nice quote was taken from van Maanen (eds.) (1983).

techniques. This is also called a 'multi-method' approach. We touched upon this issue early in Chap. 5 when talking about the principle of triangulation.

A.1.1   Introduction

It may appear somewhat bizarre to a novice in the field of methodology for whom the most obvious choice might be a 'natural' fusion of the two approaches so that their respective strengths and weaknesses can be compensated. One could easily claim that this 'double-methodology' approach should be advocated in order to achieve easily justifiable and useful applied research. Careful and alternating use of both research approaches can indeed offer valuable insight, more opportunity for the development of hypotheses, an improved comprehension of existing theoretical insights and, what is more, a direct practical benefit. Or to quote Bryman: "... in the end when quantitative and qualitative research are jointly pursued, much more complete accounts of social reality can ensue" (1988, 126). Still one should bear in mind that both methodologies come from two different traditions reflecting antagonistic views about how research should be conducted. Even studies that show examples of the fusion of both approaches, rarely accord them equal or nearly equal weight. Most researchers primarily rely on one methodology and a couple of associated methods and back-up their findings with a method (or even a technique) associated with another methodology. Despite this practice we are still convinced that combining methodologies – even though difficult – has added value. A key success factor is an alternating step-wise use of quantitative and qualitative approaches (see Chaps. 4 and 5) throughout the process of your research and the successive application of methods, techniques and criteria. We distinguish three phases in a research process: (1) Observing and deducing, (2) Theorising and conceptualising and (3) Interpretation and application. Each of these phases can be designed in such a way that a particular methodology is more predominant.

A.1.2   Phase 1: Observing and Deducing

Any researcher confronted with an organisational problem initially has little knowledge of what this problem is all about. Moreover, as pointed out in the previous chapters, the way a problem is situated on the organisational agenda is not only determined by functional, but also by political (power) and emotional considerations. Therefore, at the start of his research, the researcher should have an open attitude to the problem and the organisation. He should start with only a limited number of sensitising concepts and leave any other theoretical 'luggage' at home. This way he will become properly acquainted with the problem as he carries out his work. For example, he may (if relevant) do a number of nightshifts, attend several carefully chosen meetings, conduct a series of (open) interviews, regularly lunch at

Fig. 5.5 Quantitative and
qualitative research combined

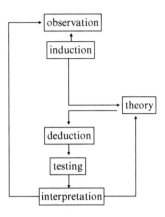

the company's canteen or accompany salesmen in the field for several days. We can hardly call it a design but choosing different 'data-sources' (observations) at different moments in time from different people would fit the bill. For convenience's sake, this could be called the first 'phase' of a research and can be typified as 'open observation'. The researcher attempts to get to know the organisation and the related problem as objectively and extensively as possible. As has been shown, this phase can be elaborated into various sub-phases and diverse methods and techniques can be used to structure the collection of the predominantly qualitative data. On the basis of these findings, the researcher can formulate a problem definition together with the people in the organisation. In theoretical-methodological terms this definition is based on an inductive empirical cycle. The researcher completes an entire qualitative research phase, in a period of 2 or 3 weeks (or even less). The essential objective remains to carry out the research in a methodologically justifiable way. He will then utilise the problem definition that he has formulated to start looking for suitable theoretical support. That marks the beginning of the second phase (Fig. 5.5).

A.1.3   Phase 2: Theorising and Conceptualising

Theory is very useful when classifying a multitude of observations: it sharpens the mind and helps to focus. It gives the research a structured framework for analysis, provided that is that the researcher has found those theoretical components that really help him progress. Although this sounds rather easy-going it demonstrates that 'theorising' is not something that can be done in a twinkling of an eye. Many researchers set out without having a clear idea in mind of how they are going to address the problem. Consequently, theory might come second and will often be degraded to a chapter in a report that is hardly read by anyone. For us theory is not something secondary, but a way to clarify a question and put it into the right perspective. Theory can help define why a problem occurs in an organisation and why it is discussed. In addition, it helps to pinpoint various aspects and their mutual relationship. It also assists in the development of alternatives for the problem and to understand its content. Moreover, it helps the researcher to confront his experiences with the experiences of others who have the same problem. Searching for theory provides ample opportunity to tap into a body of knowledge in a specific field. Often that is really quite exciting. In short: theorising supports the systematic examination of a problem in order to be able to continue researching it. On the basis of this 'confrontation' the researcher is able to develop a (preliminary) conceptual model that does not only relate to the theory involved, but also to the organisation concerned. If it is elaborated by means of a quantitative approach, it will result in sound testing. Obviously, all methodological and technical 'rules' will need to be taken into account in order to achieve a justifiable result. Working in this manner will lead to an empirical cycle that is deductive by nature. If elaborated by means of a qualitative approach it might for example lead to a fully developed conceptual model. It should be clear that once again the appropriate methodological rules, etc. are applicable here. When following this approach the empirical cycle is inductive by nature.

A.1.4   Phase 3: Interpretation and Application

Testing leads to a set of numerical data. After these data have been statistically analysed, it is once again the researcher who will need to interpret them. He can choose to do this on his own. He also has the opportunity to choose a method that involves people from the organisation. Such an analytical approach can stimulate the development of ideas about usefulness and applicability. The interpretation of data (of whatever kind) is by definition a subjective matter. Something like 'objective interpretation' does not exist. Data can only be interpreted when applying theory through the eyes of those involved. So where does it leave you as a researcher? You have the obligation to work carefully and produce applicable results. Please reconsider the array of methodical possibilities you have at your disposal. Choose carefully and you don't necessarily need to restrict your choice to one approach. You can analyse the same data using different approaches and then compare. Yes, this is multi-method analysis.

A.1.5   Combining the Best of Both

It must be clear now that in applied research the boundary between qualitative and quantitative research is in rather thin. This line between can be smudged even further. In Chaps. 4 and 5 we introduced two methodological traditions; two distinct different ways of doing research. However in order to be 'academically bullet-proof' research often ought to be a combination of both. It is possible to start the research with a qualitative approach. The result of the first phase is a number of hypotheses. In a second phase these hypotheses are put to the test according to a quantitative tradition. Based on the outcomes of this part, the research process is then finalised with a qualitative section in which the conclusions are presented in such a way that they are understandable and actionable by people in the organisation. In this way both approaches supplement each other.

A.1.6 Using the Nature of the Question for a Multi-method Approach

In Chap. 3 we strictly combined the position of looking through the eyes of the researcher with quantitative methods. In Chap. 4 we approached research while looking through the eyes of someone else with applying qualitative research methods. The rather rigid elaboration of these two positions was done on purpose since arguing in this way allows us to clearly describe the differences of both approaches, thus providing a compact overview of the line of reasoning and its consequences. In this Interlude we have already played down the differences and argued that both traditions can very well be part of one and the same research design. Still, really applying a multi-method requires expertise on the part of the researcher. It might therefore be handy to approach the issue from a different angle and start thinking in other terms. Instead of combining method and techniques derived from different traditions we also have the possibility to combine the research question once we know its nature. This makes it possible to see through somebody else's eyes and yet still maintain the position of looking through the eyes

		Paradigm choice	
		Looking through the eyes of the researcher	Looking through the eyes of someone else
Research question format	Closed research question	Cell 1	Cell 3
	Open research question	Cell 2	Cell 4

Fig. 5.6 Nature of the question combined

of the researcher. What we suggest is combining an open and closed research question (Fig. 5.6).

Cell number one comprises a closed question and looking through the eyes of the researcher. The position seems to be the traditional neo-positivistic position. Cell number four looks like the opposite: the interpretative tradition. In both cells, however, it will be possible to use either quantitative or qualitative methodologies or methods or combine them. We can describe cell number two as the situation in which the researcher is looking through his own eyes with an open research question: an inductive way of doing research leading to an explorative research. Cell number three is a position in which the researcher has decided what and how to research, yet the people in the organisation involved decide how to proceed (and yes, this turns into a kind of action research – see Chap. 5). This classification is a bit more complex. It can be understood best by studying the difference between quantitative and qualitative research first. Otherwise you might get lost.

Although fundamentally different, qualitative and quantitative research are not opposites – we do not support that academic debate. When it comes to applied research they are even complementary. Just one little quote from another source: "One of the most obvious senses in which this may occur (is): qualitative research may act as a source of hunches or hypotheses to be tested by quantitative research." (Bryman 1988, p. 134). Of course, it is the researcher's responsibility to consider the possibilities that a combined use of these two approaches offer. In making this assessment he should also take into consideration his own competencies, research experiences and any other important conditions (e.g. time, money, access). The above presented line of reasoning which can be summarised as 'inductive – deductive – inductive' briefly show that in essence each research project makes use of both the qualitative and quantitative approach. Deliberately using these approaches in an alternating way improves the quality.

References

Brewer, J. & Hunter, A. (2006). *Foundations of multi-method research: synthesizing styles*. London: Sage.

Bryman, A. (1988). *Quantity and quality in social research*. London: Routledge.

Creswell, J. W. (2008). *Research design, qualitative & quantitative approaches*. London: Sage.

Jick, T. D. (1983). *Mixing qualitative and quantitative methods: triangulation in action*. In J van Maanen (Ed.) Qualitative methodology. Newbury Park, CA: Sage.

Murray, T. & Murray Thomas, R. (2003). *Blending qualitative and quantitative methods in theses and dissertations*. London: Sage.

Chapter 6
Assessing Your Research

Working with Requirements that Determine the Quality of the Applied Methodology(ies)

Abstract Thorough research needs to meet certain criteria. We define what these criteria are, what they relate to and what role they play in the different phases of a research. The ensemble of these criteria is outlined in this chapter. After clarifying the nature of these criteria and requirements, a further distinction will be made between qualitative and quantitative research. Finally, the question will be answered as to who uses which criteria when and what this means to the researcher and his project.

6.1 Introduction

An introduction about research methodology is not complete without discussing the 'requirements' or 'criteria' the research will need to comply with. This sounds almost self-evident but when taking a tour in the methodology section of the nearest (academic) library you will soon discover that a neat overview of criteria – let alone some form of comparison – is hard to find. The question as to what are the 'right' (appropriate) criteria and how these should be dealt with initially seems again simpler than it actually is. One could say that the proper application of suitable criteria is a requirement,[1] a prerequisite for any decent research. Using these

---

[1]Requirements are: need, wish, demand, want, necessity, essential, prerequisite or stipulation. It regards an action, ability, or quality as due from (someone) by virtue of their position. So requirements are linked to a person and how he acts. This has to do with issue such as professionalism and integrity. Criteria are: a principle or standard by which something or someone may be judged or deciding upon. It literally means 'means for judging' (see for these definitions any decent dictionary). Criteria can formally be seen as independent from the actual research acts of a researcher. Although all this holds through in practice, the distinction between the two is a bit more blurred as you will notice when reading this chapter.

J. Jonker and B. Pennink, *The Essence of Research Methodology*,
DOI 10.1007/978-3-540-71659-4_6, © Springer-Verlag Berlin Heidelberg 2010

requirements and criteria enables the researcher to justify[2] the reasons for choosing a particular methodology and subsequent methods and techniques for his research. This justification can take place at three moments during the actual research process: (a) at the start of the research or (b) during the research and (c) after the research. In addition, a researcher will almost certainly have to justify his results to different stakeholders: the external client being for example (a group of) people who have to work with the outcomes of the research and the 'scientific community' or internal client, such as the supervisor or fellow students.

Conducting proper research implies the careful choice and application of criteria which relate to the nature of the research and therefore provide information about its quality. To put it simply: research should be conducted 'thoroughly'. This implies it must be efficient, methodologically justifiable, produce useful results, as well as respond to the client's needs and extend his knowledge and his possibilities to act. All this can be detailed in an endless list of all sorts of possible criteria, many of which the researcher (just starting out) will be unaware, let alone able to choose between or apply. In order to keep things workable this list of requirements is reduced to two 'main streams': *scientific* and *practical* requirements. Below a shortlist of criteria for each of these two streams can be found.

The above overview is not complete, but it is sufficient to show that there are criteria and requirements of many sorts, colours and sizes. Choosing criteria is obviously not something that should be done when the research is finished. In the remainder of this chapter we focus the attention on what these criteria are, to what and how they are related and how they play a role in the (different phases of) research. By means of the distinction made between qualitative and quantitative research, guidelines will be provided as to the choice of criteria given a specific methodological approach. The bottom-line of the chapter is to demonstrate how these criteria 'steer' the research design and -process.

Box 6.1: Criteria for Judging Research

Scientific criteria: truth, testability, controllability, objectivity, precision, consistency, reliability, repeatability, validity, the way terms are being made operational, etc.

    Practical criteria: relevancy, grounded in practice, comprehensiveness, in time, affordable, considering sensitivities and interests, completeness as far as the described problems are concerned, usability, etc.

---

[2]To justify is show or prove to be right or reasonable. A justification provides grounds, reason, basis, rationale, premise, rationalization, vindication, explanation; defense, argument, apologia, apology, case (see same source and also Chap. 8).

6.2 Juggling with Requirements and Criteria

Let's start with an everyday example. Anyone who is driving a car can constantly monitor the speed by looking at the speedometer. The speedometer measures how fast the car is moving in relation to the road. The criterion that enables this measurement to be made is the road that is (obviously) not moving. In addition, there are the traffic regulations that indicate the maximum speed which is allowed in certain situations (e.g., 50 km within a housing area). The driver of a four-wheeled motorised vehicle is authorised to drive the car, as he proved that he is able to handle this criterion by attending a driving school and passing the driving test successfully. In short, he fits the requirements. This is a recognisable situation. Yet, what this example does not clarify is that although the driver may maintain the speed limit of 50 km per hour, there is an characteristic of the situation which remains unknown: the condition of the road, street, or district (in brief, the context) in which he drives. When there are children playing in the streets, cyclists passing by, a market going on or whatever, it is foolish or even dangerous to keep to the authorised speed. Any sensible person knows that. It simply means that a criterion only functions when it is used wisely, in other words, a criterion has a functional and context-bound place in the research. This requires from the researcher the ability to apply a criterion at the right time, the right place and in a proper manner. This is determined by, among other things, the nature of the question ('open' or 'closed'), the nature of the (initially chosen) methodology and the phase of research at that moment. What is more, capable application also provides information about the way the researcher is handling the research and thus about the quality of the researcher's research actions.

6.2.1 Classification of Criteria

After the previous explanation, it should be clear that requirements and criteria are not 'something' just attached to research, a kind of 'add-on' applicable at any moment in time. While the criteria tell us something about the actual research, the way criteria and requirements are handled are indicative for the level of professionalism of the researcher. What complicates the matter here is that they can play a different role at different moments during the process of research. Therefore, dealing with criteria demands classification. Such classification is made here by distinguishing three stages in the research: (a) in advance, (b) during or (c) after the research. Examples of criteria for each of these stages are given below.

6.2.2 In Advance

If the research starts with a *closed* question, the researcher develops a conceptual model (see Chap. 3), which is then operationalised. During the conceptualisation and operationalisation of the model, it is common to check with regard to various forms of validity: the degree to which the conceptual model accurately reflects the specific theoretical concept(s) that the researcher is attempting to measure (also see Glossary). In line with many others we call this construct validity. Construct validity is one-to-one linked to *content* or theoretical validity: are the theoretical notions and concepts used providing an accurate and truthful representation of the dedicated body of knowledge in a particular domain. Please bear in mind that construct and content validity both apply to a kind of a-priori thinking; it tells us something about how the researcher creates a construct of the problematic reality. As such it does not tell much about how the actual research is carried out – if this is done in a valid way.

If the research project starts with an *open* question, a particular methodology is chosen in which both people in the organisation and the researcher find appropriate ways to carry out the research together. The research starts with several sensitising concepts: theoretical notions that guide the way of observing reality (see Chap. 5). To carry out valid research it is highly important that the participating people are not only familiar with these notions but that they are also meaningful to them. They need to meet what are commonly called the requirements of 'comprehensibility' and 'traceability' and communicability. Are the introduced notions described in such a way that they can be readily understood? For whose benefit have they been developed? It goes without saying that choosing the proper language is vital here – it is all in the words. This places quite a different emphasis on the capabilities of the researcher. Here he is required to link into the organisational vocabulary and discourse without losing the aim of the research.

> **Box 6.2: Exercise Regarding Market Opportunities**
> Look at the following question: 'Does the market of do-it-yourself tools offer an opportunity to introduce …?' (Fill in something you think is applicable). Answer the following: (a) which requirements do you think the (external) client will make? and (b) which requirements do you think that the tutor of an undergraduate project will make?
>
> Discuss, formulate and explain: Which requirements will you make as a researcher? To what extent do they coincide (or not) with one of the two (or both) stakeholders above?

6.2.3 During

The researcher will design and apply a 'measuring instrument' for his closed question (for example a questionnaire). It is with this instrument that he will, sooner or later, measure the phenomenon to be examined. Therefore, it is important that the instrument is able to measure what it is supposed to measure. Specific quality requirements monitor the standard of the instruments the researcher applies.

Again we talk about construct validity but now it applies to the construction of the instrument. At the same time, it becomes important to account for the way the researcher employs the instrument. How will he choose the research population (sampling?) and approach his respondents? This differs from an open research question.

After the researcher has 'dug' up a bit of information about the organisation he is researching, the first 'results' will follow in the form of some initial lines of thoughts, some observations (maybe even taken from different sources) all this supported by various (organisational) documents. It is the researcher who will select a form in which he can communicate these initial results to the people involved. The researcher can, for instance, choose from techniques such as a workshop, a brainstorm session or a kind of group session in which all people involved have the opportunity to work on one and the same document (so-called Delphi method). If that is to be the case it becomes important that the researcher can ensure that people can say what they need to say in a language (or another form) that suits them? His behaviour and the criteria he employs will be reflected in the process and techniques he chooses and play a steering role in achieving transparency, understanding or applicability for example.

6.2.4   Afterwards

A researcher who started his research with a closed question has in the meantime received two hundred of the three hundred questionnaires that he had sent out. Initially, he is content as he has a response rate of over 60%. That promises to provide a good start in terms of reliability and validity. Yet, on further consideration it appears that more than half of the respondents have not fully completed the questionnaire. How will the researcher deal with this data deficiency? If $N = 200$ at the start, decreases to $N = 50$ owing to the incomplete questionnaires, is the researcher still able to make any statements about the population? What would this mean for generalisability when associated with validity? Further analysis of the questionnaires shows that there is one dominant sub-population within the original target population that has answered most of the questions and sent back, proportionally, most of the questionnaires. What do these results signify and how will the researcher justify this? As the example shows, one can easily run into all kind of problems here, many of which could have not been tackled in advance. Solving them during the actual research process is not only a matter of competence and experience but also of means such as time, money and availability of alternatives. What also might happen is that the problems which arise are not surmountable in a technical sense. This means the researcher is confronted with a dilemma he has to solve – one way or the other.

After several months of demanding research at a company that had contracted him to investigate a particular matter (with an open question), our hypothetical researcher has to finalise the work by summarising his findings in a report. During the research he has received every possible support. Now it is a matter of formulating some neat conclusions, making appropriate recommendations and putting everything in a readable format. The most useful and fastest way (namely, with a view to finishing the graduation project as soon as possible) is to take all the material and to write the report without any interference from third parties. However, during the research, the researcher has made a great effort to involve people in the organisation. How can he realise this involvement in the last phase of his project as well? How will he ensure that the results are formulated clearly, understandably and relevantly, and the report is not written in an overly academic style?

The previous examples show that there are different criteria and requirements at different moments. Moreover, they can change in the course of research. Criteria concern the deliberate actions in research, the instruments the researcher uses and the way he deals with them and the outcomes. It should by now also be apparent that criteria depend on the methodology chosen and may differ substantially from each other or, sometimes, even clash. Anyone who strives for comprehensibility for those involved can easily become entangled with some form of validity or generalisibility! Both the researcher who starts with an open question and the researcher who starts with a closed question can strive for reliability. Nevertheless the significance of the term 'reliability' can take a completely different meaning once research is underway.

Generally, the requirements of sound research are classified according to qualitative and quantitative research (see Chaps 4 and 5). This classification has been used implicitly up till now. Below a more succinct overview is given that reflects the criteria that are usually associated with these two research traditions.

Box 6.3: Dilemmas of Conducting Research
From your previous research it has been shown that in the population examined there is one specific dominant subpopulation. During the research it became repeatedly obvious that the client attaches great importance to the involvement of this particular group in the implementation of possible changes resulting from the project you are conducting. As a researcher, how will you deal with this wish, knowing that you have a chance to get an appealing job in the organisation if you carry out the research thoroughly?

Box 6.4: Reliability?
Look again at the research question below and consider what the criterion *reliability* really means here. Opt for an *open* or a *closed* approach. "We would like to research how workload is experienced in our hospital." Present and discuss the results of your elaboration.

6.3 Quantitative Requirements

We think there are four focal questions when it comes to central criteria for this line of research: (a) What would happen if you did the research all over again? (b) Did you achieve what you wanted to achieve? (c) Are the research results applicable in the relevant situation? (d) Did you make a contribution to the body of knowledge, i.e., (existing) theory? This raises the issues of reliability and validity.

Research is only reliable if it can provide similar results a second time round. In order to enhance the reliability and subsequently to demonstrate it, 'triangulation' is used. The essence of triangulation is the application and combination of various data sources or methods in order to show that similar results can be achieved. Triangulation can be achieved by using different kinds of data (video images, interview reports, and observational data). Triangulation can also be accomplished by letting other researchers participate (for instance several interviews) and (or) by using different ways to ask the same (therefore different methods). Finally, through triangulation it is possible to examine a phenomenon in reality by means of different theories.

When you measure what you intend to measure the research is presumed to be valid. However, the question regarding validity comprises more than solely a judgement about the way of measuring. Validity also concerns research as a whole. Validity is based on an integral assessment of the extent to which empirical findings and theoretical considerations support the adequacy of the argumentation (Thomas 2006). There are many kinds of validity, such as validity of notions, construct validity, content validity, internal validity and external validity. Validity of notions: the notions employed in statements regarding the theoretical framework will need to be a correct interpretation of the (empirical) phenomena for which they are used. Internal validity: the semantic relationships that are presumed between the notions in statements of the conceptual model have to be a correct interpretation of coherences between the examined phenomena that were found in reality. External validity concerns generalisibility in terms of time, place and population.

Obviously, research should be controllable. We like to call this 'transparency'. For this purpose, the researcher will have to make the data available and accessible to the assessors – or other stakeholders if necessary. In business research this can be a complicated and even tricky criterion considering the possible accessibility, confidentiality and, thus, reliability of some data. If the utility comes into focus not only relevance is important, but also accuracy plays an essential role. The researcher should not forget for whom these results are relevant?

6.4 Qualitative Requirements

Research that is focused on finding answers to an open question has slightly different requirements. The researcher will continuously have to consider whether the answers he has found provide the information needed to elaborate his question.

Yet, he is not the only one who provides answers. The people who are involved in the research will also answer that question but might come up with different outcomes. They must at least understand which conclusions have been drawn. The value of qualitative research further increases when the researcher succeeds in making perceptible how and where he has conducted research (transparency again). Thus communicating intermediate results is essential. What is at least as important, in comparison to the quantitative research approach, is the reliability of the researcher himself. With a closed quantitative approach the researcher's role is considered to be neutral – some would even say 'instrumental'. In fact, the researcher will need to be invisible. With an open qualitative approach the researcher's role is not neutral per se. The researcher's interpretation can actually contribute to the search process but can also bias through his behaviour. This is why the researcher's reliability is explicitly emphasised.

Triangulation gets a different character in this approach. The essence of triangulation is the utilisation, inclusion and combination of different (data) sources in order to clarify *a number of* aspects of reality at the same time. A complicated criterion in this approach is when to actually stop searching? In the literature this is classified under the denominator of 'saturation'. Translated freely, saturation implies the moment in the research process when you realise that you are not hearing anything new. It is possible to explain this to the assessors of your research by means of triangulation techniques and subsequent data. When there are no aspects left to elucidate the point of saturation has been reached. This may sound a bit funny when you read it for the first time but that is really how it happens in practice. Obviously, in this rather open and qualitative approach utility plays a role, as do transferability and communicability in the critical appraisal of the research. The people who are involved in the research will have to understand the results and the researcher will need to be able to transfer these to them.

Box 6.5: Research Criteria: Qualitative and Quantitative
Listed below you will find an overview of the criteria of both quantitative and qualitative research. We left out transparency and triangulation since both approaches have these in common – although with different connotations. Focus in particular on the differences in the nature of these requirements and consider how you will deal with these differences in your own research.

Quantitative	Qualitative
Reliability	Saturation
Validity	Traceability
Controllability	Transferability
Repeatability	Understandability
Testability	Utility
Accuracy	Reliability
Generalisability	Communality

6.5   Responsibility Assessment

As indicated earlier in this chapter, learning how to make deliberate and careful use of these criteria and requirements can be difficult. Assessing what is 'good' research is irrevocably a job that is carried out by three 'parties': the researcher, the external client (company, external supervisor of a graduation project etc.) and the internal client (tutor of a graduation project etc.). Formulated in this way, it seems as if judging the research is a matter of an 'appraisal game' with three (un) equal parties. Unfortunately, this is not the case. The internal client often has the experience (or even substantial experience) in guiding research projects and has, therefore, developed his own preferences about what he discerns to be good research. This implies that at the start of the research, once the question has been defined, the internal client will already have a fairly complete idea of how the research should be put together and carried out, including its requirements. The researcher who has not yet had time to define the research question will not know how to put together the research, which requirements are involved and what these will mean for his work.

On the other hand, there is the external client. Once the question has been assigned, there is only one dominant criterion that occurs at different moments (particularly towards the ending of a graduation project): 'What can we do with it?' Can we use it? Will it produce something that is valuable? Of course, the external client also attaches great importance to a thorough realisation of the research. However, this is based on the assumption that possible results will need to be presented to the internal problem owners. In this respect, the term 'thorough research' has a 'political' meaning and plays a role in actually implementing the results ("We were able to conduct thorough research thanks to by... (fill-in name of the institution); this is the result and we have to use it somehow. We cannot ignore it.")

The researcher moves between those two parties armed with his own expectations, knowledge, ambition and interpretations. Sometimes he agrees with both parties, sometimes he doesn't and wants to stick to his own line of reasoning. What can also happen is that one of the two parties is extremely dominant. This may lead to the dilemma of whom to respond to. Whatever the situation, conducting research is not simple. In many cases it forms the end of a study and often is a first intense (professional) confrontation with organisational practice. And above all the research needs to be of such a quality that it is possible to complete the thesis or dissertation on time. It should come as no surprise that many students will experience difficulties in dealing with these issues at times. Sometimes the external client provides such an attractive environment that the researcher becomes totally absorbed in the company. The student may be offered a job before he has graduated and subsequently the research changes from a main priority to a side issue. 'Graduating fast' then becomes a phrase that is often used. Yet, the bottom line is that the external client does not assess the academic quality. In the end, it is the internal client who determines whether the research project is of sufficient quality – whether individually, with his colleagues, or via a board of examiners or another institution that monitors quality. It is the internal client who holds the 'power' to grant permission to get the certificate or diploma.

What should the researcher do? How can he deal with the predicament in a practical way when he still probably lacks experience? Well, for starters by constantly asking questions and carefully listening to the answers. Who defines the various requirements and are both clients aware of what these requirements imply? Have they discussed their requirements with each other and have they reached an agreement about them? If not, the researcher can stimulate it. Besides, the researcher can look into the requirements that accompany the question – and everything that has been previously said about it in terms of methodology, method and technique – taking his personal preference and basic attitude into account. It will involve serious investigation using the relevant literature and also conversations with the internal and external client throughout the research project. These conversations should be deliberately aimed at discussing the requirements and its possible changes. It is the explicit responsibility of the researcher to encourage such talks, to make notes about different perspectives at different moments in time in the form of memos, to confer with other undergraduates, or ask for the opinion of other tutors (regardless of whether they are directly involved with the work or not). Such exchanges offers opportunities to shape and document the search process and help to deliberately apply the requirements and criteria that the research demands from the researcher. Actually acting upon such findings is all part of conducting thorough research.

Box 6.6: Changing Requirements During your Research
On the basis of a closed question you have started to work on a conceptual model for a research project. The more you delve into the subject, the more you discover that you are not at all clear about where the content is going, let alone if you are in a position to elaborate it as it should be. The further you go, the more you have your doubts about the nature of the initial question. Your external and internal clients are convinced that the problem definition that has been jointly established will enable you to design a research approach that leads to a questionnaire. How will you handle this? Are you not making a serious mistake yourself? Are you observing the situation properly? How will you handle this dilemma?

6.6   Criticism

It should in the meantime be clear that both the qualitative and quantitative research approaches comprise a tremendous variety of requirements that are not always easily combined. Conducting accurate research based on one – or both – traditions (see Interlude II) is not simple. Combined with the demands of the internal or external client the researcher could soon find himself in a 'methodological minefield'. These criteria also provoke some criticism (see also points of criticism at the end of Chaps 4 and 5). We list what we think is important.

6.6.1 Quantitative

- Testing hypothesis.
- Striving for validity and reliability narrows down 'the reality' into something that is primarily measured by 'instruments' such as conceptual models elaborated into questionnaires.
- Questionnaires can be 'manipulated' perfectly by the researcher, as well as by the respondents.
- Conceptual models are primarily a (simplified) interpretation of a complex situation in reality; therefore we should not attach too much value to them.
- Requirements of quantitative research predominantly concern the tools and their construction; the actual behaviour, thinking and intentions of people can never be measured by means of these tools.
- Quantitative research leads by definition to an instrumental and non-human approach.
- As a researcher you only know if something has been implemented in a valid way after the research has been concluded. By that time you will be gone and have no say in the matter.

Box 6.7: Communication Problems
An organisation has a vivid internal communication problem. You are asked to design and conduct research into this problem.

(a) Substantiate a quantitative approach and explain clearly which requirements accompany this approach.
(b) Substantiate a qualitative approach and explain clearly which requirements accompany this approach.

Subsequently, compare the requirements that both approaches entail and with which you are confronted as a researcher. Provide a thorough analysis on the basis of this comparison. Where does it lead you as a researcher? How are you going to justify your choice? Does it correspond with your known basic attitude?

6.6.2 Qualitative

- Constructing hypothesis.
- Striving for understandability can cause the researcher to be accused of being subjective, so, by definition not academic.
- Operating on the basis of the saturation criterion provides more information about the researcher then about the collected data.
- Striving for applicability is not improved by a qualitative approach, as the researcher can hardly contribute his expertise to the research.

- Operating on the basis of qualitative data taken from different sources makes the comparison of these data almost impossible.
- Indeed, striving for a vague variation of reliability is the only thing the researcher can do, for hard facts are lacking.

It does not take much effort to extend the points of criticism discussed above, yet this is pointless. What is important is that the researcher clearly knows that no research approach is perfect. However, it cannot be denied that in general the scientific community has a distinct preference for quantitative research. This preference can be explained historically and supported by what are considered to be the top-ranking journals. But does this preference sufficiently relate to all studies that focus on business in research? It is, of course, possible to advocate a more trans- or interdisciplinary approach that is partly intertwined when choosing a multi-methodology strategy. Yet, saying all this in, e.g., a research proposal does not automatically imply doing as well – and doing it properly. Therefore, we finish with a word of advice:

- Start with a restricted number of clear and manageable criteria
- Apply them systematically (and make this approach clear as well)
- Only let go of them if changes in the research make it absolutely necessary
- In short, research should adhere to the KISS principle (Keep It Simple, Stupid)

6.7   Chapter Summary

This chapter discussed the criteria and requirements of sound research.

- A distinction has been made between 'scientific requirements' and 'practical requirements'; applied research deals with both.
- Criteria have been distinguished according to the different phases of research (in advance, during and afterwards).
- This distinction makes it clear that there are different criteria at different times and these can actually change during the course of research.
- Requirements may concern what the researcher is doing, the instruments he uses and the way he deals with the results – competencies, experience and degree of professionalism have to be mentioned here.
- Criteria and requirements may differ or in certain situations even clash depending on the methodology, methods and techniques chosen.
- Subsequently, an overview was provided of the criteria for qualitative or quantitative research.
- Whatever the chosen approach, transparency and triangulation are always part of it.
- Finally, details were provided regarding the parties involved in the appraisal of the (conducted) research: the researcher, the external client and the internal client.

The chapter concluded with a critical discussion of criteria and requirements that relate to both qualitative and quantitative research.

References

Arbnor, I. & Bjerke, B. (1997). *Methodology for creating business knowledge*. London: Sage.

Brewer, J. & Hunter, A. (2006). *Foundations of multi-method research: synthesizing styles*. London: Sage.

Collis, J. & Hussey, R. (2009). *Business research: a practical guide for undergraduate and postgraduate students* (3rd ed.). New York: Palgrave McMillan.

de Groot, A. D. (1969). *Methodology: foundations of inferences and research in the behavioral science*. The Hague: Mouton.

Millar, G. & Dingwall, R. (eds). (1997). *Context and method in qualitative research*. London: Sage.

Robson, C. (2002). *Real world research*. Oxford: Blackwell Publishers.

Thomas, A. B. (2004). *Research skills for management studies*. London: Routledge.

Thomas, A. B. (2006). *Research concepts for management studies*. London: Routledge.

Chapter 7
Acting and Organising

A Theoretical Exploration of Methodology as a Specific Form of Action

Abstract In the preceding chapters a description was provided of how to proceed in designing and conducting applied research in an organisation. By means of the fundamental distinction 'observing through the eyes of the researcher' or 'observing through the eyes of someone else' two principally different research paradigms have been set out. These paradigms comprise a huge diversity of research methodologies and methods, as well as techniques, as has been demonstrated. However, the question as to 'what is methodology' has only been answered in part. To make up for this deliberate omission so far this chapter contains a theoretical exploration of the notion 'methodology'. Therefore, we will introduce two additional 'families' of methodology namely design- and intervention methodology. Together with the described approaches to research methodology this will offer a more elaborate view. Furthermore, this view will be connected with the notion of 'acting' on the one hand and 'organising' on the other.

7.1 Introduction

Until now, this book has focused on methodologies needed for conducting research. In this respect, the question as to what methodology is seems to have been answered; methodology is associated with a specific kind of behaviour (in terms of thinking and acting) we call research. An obvious and already provided meaning is 'an explicit way of structuring one's thinking and actions in terms of research' (see Glossary). A research methodology based on a specific way of perceiving reality *indicates* the assumptions, criteria, rules and requirements the researcher needs to choose from and comply with in order to produce results that are obtained in a transparent way. We then call these results reliable and valid. How the researcher makes his choices, his line of reasoning, what he leaves out, and how he handles specific issues all lead to a contextualised research design.

Methodology can also be understood as creating an 'action protocol or doctrine' based on how the researcher does (or does not) do certain things, the order in which these things have to be conducted all associated with requirements and criteria steering the actual process of research. Criteria can be used in order to make justifiable statements about the nature and the quality of actions and results (see also Chap. 8). In this way, the action protocol in research prescribes which research activities in which order may lead to a specific desired (research) result. This assumes causality[1] in one's actions. As long as the researcher – within the framework of a chosen methodology, etc. – makes use of the appropriate methods and techniques the result will be 'valid' fundamental or applied knowledge. Using specific methodologies for varying purposes is as normal to any science domain as sleeping, eating and breathing for humans. Therefore, methodology should be considered the centre of (any) scientific action. Everything that does not pass the test of methodology will be deemed unscientific and can be disregarded. In this respect, knowledge that has been generated in a methodologically justifiable way will be given the qualification 'scientific approval'.

Apart from being deliberately naïve, the above description of methodology is a highly simple and incorrect perspective of matters. It is naïve, as it narrows down the meaning – and by that the scope – of methodology to one specific form of action that is solely focused on conducting research. Implicitly this assumes that there is only one (sometimes even dominant) methodology – a kind of 'one size fits all' approach. In the preceding chapters it has been demonstrated that this is not to be the case. Filing down methodology to a contextualised research design shows the freedom to act of the researcher. This freedom to act becomes especially discernible within the framework of research acting from a multi-methodical perspective (see Interlude II). Moreover, the assumption that methodology is only focused on conducting research is incorrect in as far as it pushes the essential meaning of methodology – being a guideline for action – to the background. From a broader angle methodology should be seen as the systematic analysis and understanding of different kinds, different 'families' of action. More specifically, thinking about methodology in a broader sense explores the why, the how and the wherefore of a particular question or questions, as well as the aims and means of a particular methodology or even a school of thought. Defined in this way it is infinitely richer in terms of scope and depth than at first thought. Adapted from a sentence by Foley (2005).

This chapter considers methodology from this broader perspective although we still limit ourselves to organisations. It should be clear that we think methodology does not always form the exclusive responsibility universe of the researcher but includes structuring, respectively changing *actions* of people in organisations. In this way, methodology is explicitly considered to be a theory of action[2] focused

---

[1]Causality refers to the assumption between a certain cause and its effect. Most common is the causality where there is an assumed strict linearity between the act itself and the (desired) effect taking place over time. This slightly naïve way of thinking can be complemented with causality in a reversed order, across time, by incident (serendipity) and so forth.

[2]For those interested in this line of thinking there is a highly sophisticated collection of English articles edited by Alfred R. Mele called 'The Philosophy of Action" published by Oxford University Press, 1997 (reprinted 2003). If you master French you can take a look at "Entre

here on organising. This expended perspective on methodology may well involve conducting 'proper' research in different organisational settings, but it may also provide the principles, prescriptions, regulations and instruments to shape and design an organisation (in part or as a whole) or carry out specific interventions[3] in that situation with the intention to improve or change. We think a kind of three-way perspective exists in which the additional perspectives are indicated tentatively as (a) 'design methodology' and (b) 'intervention methodology' in addition to (c) 'research methodology'. In order to be able to further elaborate this perspective, it is useful to start making some comments on 'acting'.

Box 7.1: A Simple Exercise Regarding Everyday Acting
Which actions are necessary to fry an egg properly? Carefully describe the necessary actions and the proper order of things to achieve the desired result (which is determined by your criteria). If necessary, make a diagram of the different steps and look at the 'compelling' order of the steps. And no, it is not possible to fry an egg if the pan is not placed on the gas yet, regardless whether you have lit the gas or not!

7.2   Acting

It is impossible for humans not to act. Laying, sitting, standing or walking, talking or being still, opening doors or closing them, looking or not trying to look: you are always doing something since it is impossible to do nothing. When acting is understood in the sense of organising and change, in processes that also implicate the actions of others, then humans act from the beginning to the end, day in day out with a certain intention[4] in mind. One has to decide to act also when the decision is not to act. Acting implies: "intentionally intervening in the flow of events with which the actor (e.g. researcher, advisor, employee, housewife, manager, and

---

Dire et Faire" a collection of essays written by Daniel Sibony, published in 1989 by Grasset (Paris). Both works are to be considered for the advanced reader though.

[3]Intervention, literally meaning 'coming in between', refers to the deliberate act or series of consecutive acts of someone in a specific situation with the intention to alter that situation according to e.g. an overall plan, concept, model, norm or anything else. Intervening changes the course of events and, conversely, the course changes the action. By intervening differences are realised. Any intervention is by definition normative. Interventions can be realised through (dedicated) instruments – previously referred to as methods and techniques. Acts are, therefore, instrumental.

[4]The notion of 'intention' points at the assumption that when an act is deliberate this deliberateness is based upon the act itself and a supposed effect. This is one to one linked to the notion of causality. Yet, when introducing 'intention' it assumes that the actor has the knowledge (the so-called 'savoir-faire') to choose an act and either have himself or others act upon this chosen act with a specific goal – the original intention – in mind.

author) – the one who acts – is confronted. By acting, actors bend...this flow to their will" (Hoekstra 1992). Acting takes place in a specific social context we call organisations; one that is (re) produced by and through actions. The most problematic here are the acts themselves since acting can take different forms and shapes and also because deliberate non-acting is also a manifestation of acting.

People (re) construct and (re)produce their own (social) environment in and through their actions and interactions[5] with others. The environment is created as a co-production of people and their actions. Human interaction runs the risk of becoming incomprehensible if one assumes the context to be stable, ambiguous and not social by nature. Any social environment is ambiguous, plural and above all social-dynamic. Acting is an intentional attempt to organise that environment, to exert influence on it in order to obtain, e.g. influence or a desired order. Organising from a research methodology perspective comprises observing, examining, assessing and intervening in those organisations that we produce and (re)discover as assignments, ambitions or problems in and by our acting. The organising itself – seen as a bundle of acts and interactions based on intentions – can take place from an individual or (deliberately chosen) collective perspective. Observed from this perspective organising will continuously change and is subject to constant change as a result of its fundamental social-dynamic character.[6] Organising never stands still.

The path that should be taken when organising demands paying attention to certain things such as influence (cause-result assumption), effect (impact), durability, time and overall coherence. At the same time, this requires and assumes a form of conceptualising of the individual's own role and position. Making deliberate choices is something typically human. Choosing means doing things and not doing other things. It entails acting with a certain intention. In this way, 'not choosing' can also be considered a certain form of 'choosing'. Making a choice for a specific direction or a goal requires insight into one's own influence in order to distinguish the intention of one's own action in creating and maintaining what is being organised. This is organising that does not only need to concern 'the organisation' and its functional requirements, but also – more broadly speaking – take into consideration the talents, capabilities and abilities of each person. From this perspective, the process of developing and learning, acquiring new knowledge and skills, can be considered as the development of a personal action repertoire. It is in the act of acting that people learn mostly through trial and error and, thus,

---

[5]Again we touch upon an intriguing notion here. Interaction can be defined as the (ongoing) acts or actions between actors based on those acts. It is in the stream of ongoing events that actors act and interact on the basis of each other's acts. For those interested: Karl Weick (1979) has written a landmark book on the phenomenon of organisational interactions (see references at the end of this chapter).

[6]As can be observed we take the explicit view here that organisations are fundamentally social by nature. They are created and exist because people have done so – intentionally. There are of course other views on the on ontological nature of organisations. See for an excellent overview: Morgan, G. (1997). *Images of organization,* London: Sage Publications.

discover the limits of their own capabilities and actions and subsequently their own (limited) influence on the (re)construction of a certain environment within or outside organisations.

> **Box 7.2: The Nature of Acting**
> Discuss one or more of the following statements preferably in a group. Please note: there are no right or wrong answers.
>   What do people do when they act in organisations? Can you provide examples?
>   And one step further ...
>   How is acting – aimed at designing – distinguished from acting aimed at organising? How is it expressed?
>   How is acting aimed at change distinguished from normal organisational acting? And who conducts it?

> **Box 7.3: Managerial Acting: Entrepreneurship**
> Entrepreneurs have to deal with many uncertainties. They all have their own strategy and philosophy, their own culture when trying to handle these uncertainties. Moreover, they became an 'entrepreneur', by relying on their intuition; that is what they are good at. With a purely formal system this is not feasible. So could it be that true entrepreneurship is the art of handling uncertainties? Accepting that viewpoint would make quite a few MBAs redundant.

> **Box 7.4: The Rationality of Thinking**
> "What occupies me is the idea that you think that you are thinking. You think that you steer your life by thinking. However, this is self-deception. Thinking does not exist. ... What you think in hindsight to be a rational reasoning, in reality is an emotional structure that you need for the occasion." Quoted from: De Harde Kern and Frida Vogels (1994)

7.2.1 Action Repertoire

A capability to act is expressed in one (or more) *acting repertoire(s)*. Such a repertoire provides a (pre-programmed) set of instructions about how to act in certain situations: what to do, what to say and what not to do. This is not only very handy but also mandatory to survive since no one could cross a busy street without such a dedicated repertoire. Methodically elaborated an action repertoire is an individual's collection of methods and techniques that are deemed useful to retain either on the basis of experience or cognitive conviction. 'If I do it this way, I know I will get the desired result', or 'I have learned to do it in this way' are expressions of this individual repertoire. Although the owner of the repertoire probably thinks that he is unique in his doing, it appears that such repertoires are explicitly shaped on the basis of (social) norms and other forms of societal conditioning and discipline.

A considerable part of the individual and collective learning processes is employed to produce, complete, accentuate and learn how to combine these repertoires. We frequently call this socialisation or – with a slight twist of meaning – institutionalisation. These processes can be considered as forms of discipline: learning what is allowed and what not. Once again it comes in very handy to know how to act in a specific organisation – what the 'hidden' rules are. In this process of discipline, copying and demonstrating play important roles. Therefore, the transfer of a specific action repertoire is something that has to be learned. In the course of time, we appear to have learned naturally how to act in a certain situation. Questions such as how to get up in the morning, what to do next or which words to use in a common encounter can be answered immediately by appealing to the appropriate action repertoire. This repertoire is saved in 'causal maps' or in 'screens'. A well-balanced and broad action repertoire ready to imply in a variety of situations is thus very useful. Time and again it gives clear indications of how to act – not only intentionally but also purposefully. Conducting research concerns a specific form of acting – besides organising, eating, sleeping, driving, cooking, cherishing, changing, rebuilding, collecting, gardening, laying bricks and looking – and demands a specific action repertoire. It sounds self-evident, but it is not.

7.2.2   Reflecting

Humans have the advantage that they are able to reflect on their actions and that of others – maybe it is that particular talent that distinguishes man from other living creates. "Did I handle that well?" or "Should I deal with that differently next time?' These are questions that pertain to reflection. Reflection can take place in advance or in hindsight and includes the mental or visual act of assessing actions. It goes without saying that one can reflect on one's own action and on those performed by others. Because a great part of our actions takes place seemingly 'automatically',[7] it is desirable or even wise to reflect on one's own actions every once and a while. Also because actions tend to be self-evident there is a natural inclination to prefer a specific kind within the (potential) action repertoire, because it feels familiar, it is useful, it gives a secure feeling and it is almost certain to work. We tend to stick to

---

[7]Just imagine for one moment that you have to (re)construct from scratch all the actions involved in getting up in the morning and preparing for classes.

what we know works. Over time we develop our personal preferences – nothing wrong with that. Yet, the result comes down to a tight set of all possible actions.

However, there is another reason to reflect critically and frequently on the availability or usefulness of (your own or somebody else's) action repertoire. Anyone who wants to do something will (intentionally or unintentionally) make a plan in advance. Anyone who wants to go shopping will make a list (even if only in his head). Prior to taking action it is apparently possible to reflect on the way you will act in a particular situation. In your mind you can visualise your action in the future and assess its effect beforehand: in this way, you are making a *future oriented action plan*.

Conducting research also requires careful reflection of your own actions (in advance, during and afterwards) and requires that you plan the research activities. Doing research is not a form of spontaneous or intuitive action or (especially at the beginning) a form of acting according to routine. Conducting research is a highly specific way of acting. Action planning within the context of research results in a (suitable) design (methodology, methods, etc.), reasoned by the researcher (and) (or) others involved by taking into account the nature of the research question nature and context in which it occurs.

This planning concerns taking specific actions in research and tries to anticipate problems and possibly eliminate them by appealing to (potential) solutions from complementary action repertoires. It also indicates (finally) how the researcher will try to achieve them. Action planning that has been well prepared will result in a research action plan. In this plan the researcher indicates his intentions, his interventions and the causality of steps over time all this to achieve a desired result.

When methodology is described in this way, it becomes apparent that action reading, action repertoire and action planning are all in line with each other. Moreover, it seems as if methodology not only provides the path along which to act but also to reflect on this action.[8] Implicitly it also becomes clear that acting within the context of organising actually comprises specific groups of activities such as analysing, organising, designing and changing.[9]

---

[8] Learning as a result of research can take place through the systematic use of memos (see Chap. 5) – in itself a technique. This is a fine practical example of how the individual researcher can keep track of his own line of reasoning during the process of carrying out his research. The actual learning appears over time when reading back through these memos. All of a sudden dominant themes, preoccupations and patterns will appear. That is real learning in action.

[9] Throughout this paragraph we have deliberately omitted to touch upon two scholarly debates. One concerns defining the nature of the act itself. When is an action an action? Are actions only 'physical' or is talking also an action? The second debate concerns the question as to when actions are say generic – everyday common actions – or organisational. People bring common actions to any organisational setting (they drink coffee, have lunch and talk about the weather). Where the boundary lies between those actions and specific organisational actions is hard to determine. When you meet the boss in the corridor an talk briefly about you common hobby, what kind of action is that?

Box 7.5: Discussion Regarding Everyday Acting
Draw up a list of all (or most) possible kinds of action that you can do in a normal day (for instance, think about making coffee, taking a shower, cycling and eating). When you complete the list, check to see if you can subdivide it into different criteria such as 'work', 'hygiene', 'learning', etc. Make sure your criteria are clear. Subsequently, discuss each other's list, criteria and classification (in large or small groups).

Box 7.6: Some Definitions of Acting
Acting
   Intentional intervention in the flow of events with which the researcher – the person who acts – is confronted.
   Action Repertoire
   A complex (pre-programmed) set of instructions explaining how to handle a specific situation, saved in 'causal maps' or 'frames of reference'.
   Action Plan
   A plan in which the researcher outlines the individual steps that will be taken at different moments in order to achieve a specific result.

7.3 Normal Organisational Actions in Relation to Research Action

Based on the previous section the inevitable question is how 'normal' organisational action differs from the kind of activity that has been previously indicated as 'research' action. After all, in both cases it is a matter of a dedicated action repertoire, planning and execution. We like to file down the distinction between 'normal' and 'research' action to two core elements.

7.3.1 Knowing

Anyone who is conducting research aims to find some answers. Why do Eskimos greet each other with their noses? And why do the French greet each other with three kisses? Why do the Spanish take siestas? Why do the English eat kippers for breakfast? Why do people keep driving cars despite the omnipresent traffic congestion in The Netherlands? Finding the appropriate answers to questions unanswered before the start of the research results in knowledge. This knowledge can be employed, for instance by presenting solutions, suggesting changes or by drawing up an implementation plan.[10] The product of research is a kind of knowledge (which may lead to actions) that is created on the basis of actions that are subjected to their own 'rules of the game'. The fact that 'knowing' can be expressed in different ways or may contain various meanings for different parties tends to complicate the issue. Knowing may directly concern improving an existing local action repertoire ("If we adjust this procedure in this way, we will have fewer accidents in the future"), but it may also concern a certain organisation-bound thinking technique for instance: "The research clarifies how we think about this subject." What is more, knowing may result in a collective and individual meaning that may still entail differences: "I did not know that we thought so differently about it." This shows that the relationship between 'knowing' and 'acting' is definitely not one and the same.

7.3.2 Justifying

'Justifying' concerns knowledge of a completely different kind. It is being able to prove how you obtained a particular piece of knowledge. In other words, you are able to justify the way that you obtained this knowledge. This is justification you provide to the client (the organisation that presents the problem) or to the tutor of your undergraduate project (the organisation that sees to it that you conduct your research properly). The justification – assuming that there is a problem definition, a research objective and a research question – is provided by drawing up a research plan that explains how you will take on the research, giving details of the path you wish to follow and how you will draw up and realise your research. Depending on the question's nature (open or closed) you will know this at the start of the research project. To be able to justify your research requires deliberate choices with regard to the way the research has been planned; it requires methodology, methods and techniques that suit the research. It demands requirements and criteria in order to check whether planned actions match the actions that actually took place. It requires standards in order to determine the similarities or deviations and to answer the question as to whether these are still within the 'margins'. Knowing that you have deliberately developed knowledge in a justifiable way is one of the most distinct features that distinguish common organisational acting from what we have been called research acting. As such, it clearly can be seen as a specific form of action.

---

[10]Action plans are intentionally created 'designs' to bring about change – no matter the nature of that change. What we do in such an implementation plan is to translate a-priori knowledge represented by views, opinions, models and norms into interventions creating a desired (new) situation. The change laid down in this implementation plan is mainly driven by the criterion of 'improvement', the central assumption being that change can be instrumentalised.

Box 7.7: Discussion: Methodology and Action
Discuss to what extent (and why) the statement(s) is (are) justifiable that 'methodology is similar to action' or that 'action is similar to methodology'. In preparing these statements think about all those forms of action (and acting) that have not yet been discussed. It may be useful to mention some of them in order to underline your argument.

7.3.3 Acting and Organising

If research can be defined as a special form of acting, then it is obvious that this is also possible for the notion 'organising'. In the previous sections a number of related notions have been discussed that are applicable here, too. For instance, organising is determined by intentionality, which when translated into business jargon is replaced by the term 'purposefulness'. Organising is truly social by nature, which is expressed by the continuous interaction processes between people as well as the fact that it is shaped on the basis of agreements (for the sake of clarity we will leave the term 'emotion' aside). Just as research is a *process* activity, so is organising. Moreover, an organisation can be perfectly described by referring to the set of (local) action repertoires and action plans. So, at first inspection organising and research have a lot in common.

A closer look reveals that organisations often have their 'own' specific action repertoire that is expressed in, for instance, behaviour, concepts, language and habits that are typical for one specific organisation. Typical for this repertoire is that it loses significance outside the organisation. Understanding why and how such a 'contextualised' repertoire has been created and is maintained is an exciting field of study for a vast number of people.

As a result, organising can be defined as the creation and continuous regulation of organising processes that are aimed at a variety of goals – inside and outside the organisation, individual or collective. Organising thus becomes structuring interactions and is constantly in flux. Therefore, organising involves deliberately working on change. What is more, organising creates a permanent form of change. It implies changing in the sense of creating organising processes that take place on the basis of conventions about 'what is common here', expressed in sets of action repertoires.

Box 7.8: Discussing the Nature of Organising
Just as there are a variety of research methodologies, one could advocate the creation of an organisation or organising methodology. It would be interesting to know whether such a methodological point of view would produce additional value (and insights) for the way people think about organisations and/or organising, or whether it would solely result in the development of new terminology. What do you think?

> **Box 7.9: Discussing a Methodology of Organising**
> Jointly choose a specific theory or concept about organisations respectively organising that is familiar to everyone, for example a mechanistic concept. Subsequently, discuss whether you can imagine the concept of an organising methodology and what it entails.

7.4 Design and Change

What we have brought about is a perspective on organisations in which change is an integrated part of organising. Change and organising are two sides of the same coin. The moment one starts to organise it implies creating deliberate change. This line of reasoning is certainly not common. For decades thinking about how to structure an organisation and then how to bring about change were two distinct disciplinary fields. In fact this rather artificial distinction can still be found in many educational programmes or consultancy practices. It should come as no surprise that over a long period of time, many different methods have been developed either to guide the process of structuring or bring about change.[11] Changing an organisation is based on a number of implicit or explicit assumptions and related interventions about the most effective way of organising. They again underline a specific methodology, i.e. one that entails intervention. Creating change in organisations demands a suitable intervention methodology, one that takes the social and technical side of any enterprise into account. Acting on purpose – here labelled as intervening – on the basis of these assumptions implies a dedicated methodology based on its own body of knowledge expressed in methods, tools and techniques.

The term 'change' as used academically and in daily (organisational) language is characterised by plural meanings that often result in a vague form of not being determined. Nevertheless, many articles, reports and books write about 'change' and its creation as if every colleague, consultant and manager knows exactly what it implies. This is often preceded by an almost always incomplete and symptomatic list of factors, respectively developments that boosted the need for change, for instance globalisation, digitalisation, transformation and so forth. Subsequently, the author presents his 'prescription' for change without any form of theoretical explanation let alone justification. Often his recipe has been developed on the

---

[11]Although tempting we refrain here from really touching upon literature in the field of organisational change. For those interested take a look at for example: Cummings, T. G. en Worley, C. G., (2001) *Essentials of Organization Development & Change*, South-Western College Publishing, Cincinnati, Ohio (VS); Huczynski, A., (1987) *Encyclopaedia of Organizational Change Methods*, Gower (GB) or Jonker, J., (1995) *Toolbook for Organizational Change: A practical approach for managers*, Van Gorcum, Assen – just to name a few publications.

basis of a limited number of case studies and mixed with his 'seasoned' experience and authority. The accompanying argumentation supporting his results is often along the lines: 'This has succeeded in practice; it is effective and therefore you could apply it as well'. Yet, in the huge amount of literature that has been produced about organisational change the meaning of terms such as 'changing' and 'change' remain theoretically minimally founded. It is appealing to provide a critical analysis of the existence and nature of the often-implicit methodology upon which the changing of organisations is based. Such a methodology works on the supposition that there are actors who deliberately want to or have to intervene in organisations. Changing intentionally is also based on implicit or explicit notions about 'the way to be followed' in brief: on methodological assumptions. This 'methodology' is based on a sense of order to intervene and the subsequent use of an appropriate methodology. It is common to describe the 'intervention' itself – the actual 'influencing act' (Van Beugen 1981, p. 25) – in terms of 'intervening' or interventions. Taken together, the term 'intervention methodology' consists of: 'the way in which' a 'user' of this methodology is able to realise changes intentionally by making use of interventions. This is an intervention methodology that may concern the 'hard' as well as the 'soft' aspects of an organisation. It is based on both physical and social technology and instruments that are derived from it.

Scholarly debates about change, its fundamental relation to organising and the clear methodology that has resulted are even harder to find. When considering for a moment the Research Pyramid introduced earlier as a Change Pyramid even the advanced reader will find it hard to find academic readings focussing on the methodology of change and underlying paradigms. Hoekstra wrote: "It seems as if the theoretical issue of change is carefully left in the middle or is possibly even avoided." (1992, p. 112). Twenty-five years later this situation has hardly changed.

7.4.1 Patriarch Lewin

Change in organisations is based on the ideas of Lewin (1951) since the Second World War. Lewin designed a rather mechanistic approach of the stages for change in terms of a quasi-stationary balance between factors that are stimulating and those that are slowing down. A specific quasi-stationary balance (or: steady state) can be changed by (1) 'unfreezing' the balance (unfreezing), (2) realising the desired changes (moving) in order to (3) 'freeze' the newly achieved state of balance (refreezing). Innumerable methods and techniques – and variants – have been developed in order to realise this basic pattern. Lewin's analysis describes, from a specific almost mechanistic perspective, the behaviour of people in organisations and how to approach desired change but does not analyse the change itself (also see for example Hoekstra 1992, p. 112). Change is no more than a phase in a process, but what happens there and how it happens remains hidden in a 'black box'.

7.4.2   Criticism

It is remarkable that precisely this naïve method of Lewin, this basic pattern, erroneously also called model, forms the basis for approximately nine of the ten changes. The same content can be found in organisational plans such as 'Vision 2000', 'Tracks towards change' or 'Customer First'. The evaluation of the results attained using this method always shows the same pattern: seven out of every ten change projects are not realised; if they do get off the ground they falter, get bogged down or – what frequently occurs – are caught up by new developments that require a different approach or new changes. Despite all the methodological problems attached to research into the success or failure of change processes, it may be worth questioning whether this popular method and the 'methodology' behind it, relate to the nature of change issues people face when organising.

On closer analysis, the intervention methodology for bringing about change is predominantly grounded in an instrumental solution to a fundamentally social issue; no wonder that each approach based on this perspective faces resistance. The current intervention methodology is developed from a natural science concept based upon a mechanical order of reality. Subsequently the structure of being able to know what we know and how we know it leads to a clear approach for developing knowledge about reality. In this approach a distinction into two 'basic attitudes' is assumed: an 'expert approach' versus a 'development approach'. It is possible that the last 100 years of business research have actually only served to show that (a) there is a tension between those two approaches, (b) how this tension can be more-or-less reduced respectively solved from different perspectives and (c) that the social component of this (hybrid) construction is 'harder' than structural or process aspects. Changing effectively presumes (a) a dedicated theory about action, (b) a paradigmatic concept about what organising is and (c) an (intervention) methodology that corresponds to (a) and (b). The question is how to define a suitable methodology, which elements should be taken into account and how to transfer or use these elements. This requires some serious critical reflection in order to achieve different ways of thinking in methodological terms.

7.4.3   Action and Designing

Just as one can reflect on the relationship between organising, change and action, it is also possible to reflect on designing organisations. Designing makes what needs to be organised visible. If making organisational choices is interpreted broadly, it involves establishing those sets of coherent actions that – given the nature of the product or service to be produced – are most appropriate. We tend to call this efficient (and) (or) effective. The way this is done and the accompanying presumptions and suppositions that play an important role can in a similar way, when taken together, be considered as a 'design' methodology. A design methodology concerns the way people think about shaping organisations. Designing can be defined as structuring actions on the basis of norms and criteria (for example efficiency and effectiveness) in light of certain efforts. Two 'basic attitudes' can be distinguished: a functional design approach and a social 'construction' approach.[12]

However, this book does not explicitly deal with designing and structuring organisations, as there are already excellent publications in this field. Briefly, however, what comes to light is that thinking about methodology for designing again touches upon the previously described general methodological point of reference. Moreover, it possibly underlines the fact that the researcher should be able to *deliberately* say what kind of methodology he is working with in order to do justice to the 'usefulness' requirement of applied research.

The chosen classification of methodologies is definitely not common. Whereas research methodology has a long tradition embedded in scientific theoretical developments, this is definitely not the case for design and intervention methodology. Design methodology has a tradition dating back about 100 years. On closer examination, it becomes clear that for about 70 years during this period the prevailing question was how to achieve efficient and effective functional designs. Intervention methodology has been an issue of considerable interest since the Second World War and – aligned with mainstream concepts about designing organisations – has been centred around the question of controllable change. What both traditions have in common, however, is a strong focus on technique or techniques as well as instruments.

7.5 Methodology and Technique

In a particular design change materialises thanks to the use of techniques by an actor (advisor, researcher, manager, etc.). Certainly, one can question once more whether the nature of these techniques is taken into consideration by the actor and also if these techniques have been chosen in line with a corresponding methodology and method. As a technique can be used within discriminating designs, techniques do tend to develop a life of their own. Having these techniques at your disposal will not naturally lead to sound designs respectively successful changes. Techniques are instrumental means. They will steer the action with a more or less precise description of how it should be done.[13] Applying a specific technique is not a key to dealing

---

[12]Those who are interested to better understand these two approaches are advised to read Mintzberg's landmark book called 'Structuring in Five's' first, then reed the already referred to work of Karl Weick and finally, to understand the scope of structuring possibilities between those two perspectives one could read Morgan's 'Images of Organization'. These three publications as a whole will most probably serve as an adequate introduction.

[13]Techniques can be seen as a condensed form of 'know-how' and subsequent 'know-what'. As such, they are recipes for action transferring certain savoir-faire.

properly with methodology; the choice of a specific technique is predominantly chosen on the basis of assumed causality. As a result the acting is gradually 'instrumentionalised' whereas the technique becomes a form of 'social technology' that may involve a particular way of thinking and action. Especially in the consultancy practice, it can be repeatedly observed that this 'social technology' is sold with attractive packaging as the panacea to many organisational- and change problems. The choice for suitable social technology is moreover steered by the way in which parties that are involved problematise their situation. A consequence of this practice is that dealing with problems is gradually narrowed down to buying respectively selling the social technology that appears to fit a specific situation on the basis of who is labelling best.

Similar to the introduced distinction between different sorts of methodology, it is also possible to make a distinction between design techniques and intervention techniques. For instance, design techniques are techniques that concern the (re-) structure of (organisational) processes such as Business Process Re-engineering (BPR) or the construction of a management system like ISO 9000.

Intervention techniques are those techniques that a researcher or advisor can use in order to change or improve a certain situation. Random examples are: brainstorm sessions, confrontational meetings, distributing posters, installing a buddy system, creating a top-hundred meeting and so forth.

This classification is neither 'watertight' nor exclusive. For instance, research techniques can be used as intervention techniques as well (for example the use of a group discussion technique to go over a certain problem). Moreover, the way in which a design technique can be used may uncover more information (e.g. employees describing the processes in which they are involved within the framework of redesigning them). If and how these techniques are employed depends on the method and underlying methodology, but also on the (intentional) choices that the researcher and/or advisor makes with regard to the goal he wants to achieve.

Box 7.10: Techniques Revisited
Look for a number of frequently applied techniques in (professional) literature. For instance, think about a SWOT analysis, a Life-Cycle Analysis (LCA) or the protocol for a brainstorm session (but there are tons more!). Discuss the nature of the technique and what can be said about it from the perspective of its method.

Box 7.11: Relating Techniques to a Methodology
Check whether some of the techniques you frequently use can be attributed to one (or more) of the previously described methodologies. Do you interchange them? Have you ever considered doing so?

7.6   Chapter Summary

This chapter again looked at what methodology is. Its goals were not only to look at analysing problems in organisations, but also to methodologies related to (re) designing or changing organisations. The essence has been to underline the fact that methodology is both useful in daily life and in working in organisations (in whatever role). Subsequently, a distinction has been introduced between three 'types' of methodology: research methodology, design methodology and intervention methodology. Furthermore, central notions such as action, intervention and organising where introduced, elaborated and linked to each other. The chapter as a whole provided some critical thinking in the field of methodology, on the one hand, and on organisations and change on the other.

References

Bassala, G. (2001). *The evolution of technology*. Cambridge: Cambridge University Press.
Hoekstra, M. H. R. (1992). *Doen en laten; handelingstheorie van organiseren en veranderen*. Muiderberg: Coutinho.
Lewin, K. (1951). *Field theory in social science*. New York: Harper.
Weick, K. E. (1979). *The social psychology of organizing*. London: Addison Wesley.
Weick, K. E. (1995). *Sensemaking in organizations*. London: Sage.

Chapter 8
Elaborating Your Own Research Design

Writing a Proposal, Helpful Questions and a Final Checklist

Abstract This last chapter summarises the preceding seven chapters by providing questions and checklists that can be used to prepare and conduct (individual) research. Therefore, it does not add any new knowledge or insights that have not been discussed in the previous chapters. Anyone who has limited time available to study the content of this book is advised to read the first and second chapter and depending on the nature of the research either the fourth or fifth chapter. Then, take a quick look at the sixth chapter and this last one. The chapters and interludes in-between mainly serve to consolidate the different perspectives that are being discussed. Chapter seven can be read as a kind of 'bonus' and contains a theoretical examination of the relationship between action and methodology within an organisational context.

8.1 Introduction

Conducting sound research is no sinecure. It comprises various (theoretical and methodological) pitfalls you can identify in advance. But once you think that you are on the right track all kinds of unexpected things might happen that force you to revise your plans. Moreover, different stakeholders (internal or external) make different demands that will not always coincide with each other. Assuming an open or closed question – elaborated into a research strategy and design for qualitative or quantitative research – the actual research can still be structured in fundamentally different ways. Which choices are made partly depend on features such as the personal preferences of the researcher, the time available, the requirements that are linked to the results and a considerable number of other things. Appropriate methods and techniques have to be selected carefully and consciously. It is not sufficient to just write a questionnaire or carry out some semi-structured interviews. Yet, even after careful consideration once started it may also be necessary to change the approach that has been chosen on the basis of provisional results.

J. Jonker and B. Pennink, *The Essence of Research Methodology*,
DOI 10.1007/978-3-540-71659-4_8, © Springer-Verlag Berlin Heidelberg 2010

Taken as a whole conducting research is like a Chinese juggler balancing ten plates on turning sticks. No wonder some students confronted with designing and conducting a thorough piece of research during their studies often appear unable to see the wood for the trees. Yet here the German proverb applies: "Übung macht der Meister" meaning that it is only through exercise – through doing research – one learns to know how to handle things properly.

In preceding chapters a concise attempt has been made to describe the essence of (research) methodology. With the exception of Chap. 7 – which contains a theoretical reflection about action, organising and methodology – this book has focused on all the elements and considerations that play an important role in conducting sound research. The deliberately chosen brevity does entail the risk that less time has been spent on certain subjects than they actually deserve. Fortunately, there is a wealth of existing (methodological) literature that can rectify this flaw. It is with this in mind that a list of references has been included at the end of each chapter to enable an in-depth study of these subjects.

In conclusion, all 'elements' (considerations, parts, questions, criteria etc.) that play a role in designing and conducting research will be listed here in the form of questions. These questions will be accompanied by a brief explanation and supported by a final checklist. Anyone who experiences trouble answering these questions or who wants to find out what is behind the question can return to the relevant chapters that are mentioned after each question. The questions have been deliberately numbered, in order to facilitate the task of identifying or tracing back the questions to the relevant chapter. However, this does not mean that the questions have to be answered in that seemingly compelling order. It is useful way to proceed, but not mandatory. You are free to choose the order of answering the questions in your own way. But, before moving to these questions and the final checklist, we start with an outline of a research proposal.

8.2   The Research Proposal[1]

Many academic institutes require students to write a research proposal before they actually start their research. The following remarks provide a generic guide to structure the content of your research proposal.

Working title	Describe the topic using a title and subtitle. Generally the (main) title is meant to attract attention while the subtitle provides an indication of the approach to the topic often making a reference to the methodology being used – all this in one (!) sentence.

[1]This research proposal outline was taken from the book written by Chris Hart (1998) called "Doing a Literature Review". Hart has written a couple of highly practical books for students when it comes to searching and analysing literature. We have made our own adaptation of one of the appendices he is providing.

Abstract	Snappy summary of the research topic, stating the central problem, issue or phenomenon and where the gap lays for the research you want to undertake together with an indication of what and how you want to achieve. Please be aware that writing a high quality abstract is a though job. Limit yourself to a maximum of 350 words (one page A4).
Introduction	Provides a brief yet lively introduction to the subject/problem, its context, important theoretical notions, major methodological approach, the relevance and expected results. Someone who has read your introduction should know what this research is all about and how you intend to approach it in terms of theory and methodology.
Scope	Spend a paragraph on the exact area of your research for example period of time, language (when it comes, e.g., to a literature review), subject, disciplines involved, sampling, unit of analysis (e.g., policy, programmes, activities, actual behaviours etc.). Make clear in what way and to what extend claims for generalisability can be made or what the limits are.
Aims	General statements about the intent, direction or goals of the research – where is it you want to go. Please try to specify in terms of theoretical, practical and methodological aims. Are you going to achieve results in all three domains or one or two?
Objectives	Specific, clear and to the point statements of intended outcomes from the research you will undertake, for example: search and review of literature regarding a specific topic (e.g., "The Godfathers of Management at the turn of the last Century") or a particular debate (e.g., "Who are the stakeholders and their stakes in the debate on Corporate Social Responsibility in Europe").
Justification	Provide the rationale for doing the research on the specified topic, why research needs to be done on this particular topic or problem, what the particular angle and substance is you bring to either the field of the existing body of knowledge. Make clear references to existing literature, show gaps in knowledge, the potential usefulness of a methodology you have in mind, possible benefits of outcomes (understanding, practice, policy, theory etc.) and for whom. Provide a limited number of key references to support your case and also in order to demonstrate that you are aware of the existing body of knowledge regarding the topic you want to research.
Literature	Describe briefly the history of the topic identifying landmark studies and publications indicating central arguments (pro and con) made. Demonstrate the major issues with respect to your subject or central practical problems identifying the gap you intend to look at in your research. Then indicate what will be some likely research questions (for qualitative research) or possible hypothesis (for a quantitative research). Please remember the nature of the question you introduce here. If necessary provide a limited number of key terms; why they are important, how they are defined and will be used (sometimes this can also be done in a Glossary or Thesaurus). Aim to identify what the contribution of your research will be to the existing body of knowledge as it appears through leading publications.
Methodology	A concise justification for the methodological approach (methodology and methods) you intend to employ and which data collection (one or more) and analytical technique(s) you will use. There is no need to justify and describe the methodology in-depth but justify at least the following: specify whether qualitative or quantitative and provide arguments related to the nature of the question, use of an existing approach (methodological replication), explanation why alternative methods were rejected or not, the use of specific techniques for

	data collection and analysis, anticipation of possible issues and problems and how you intend to address them.
Ethics	Indicate if you think you might encounter any ethical issues during the research project. Think of: access to data, involvement of people in the organisation, use (of publications), and confidentiality including agreements with corroborating organisations. Who owns the results of your research? Is it necessary to protect data and or people involved and what will you do to make sure this is covered?
Provisional schedule	Provide a general timetable for completing the research. Ideally, this should be broken down into manageable segments based on intermediate outcomes, indicating the task necessary to complete each assuming you will have only normal problems. Please include 'spare' time – you need to sit back and think things over.
Resources	Identify any (special) equipment you will need for example computers, software, access to (special) libraries, the use of third-party databases, cost of field visits, language editing, room rental etc. Please put the calculations for your resource requirements in an appendix. Indicate how you intend to obtain necessary funding (e.g., university, organisation, foundation).
Bibliography	This is the (brief) bibliography of all works cited in your proposal. It may include works not cited that will be followed up in the main research. Please note that there are different ways of citing references. The most commonly used presentation for social sciences is APA referencing, see below for helpful sites: http://owl.english.purdue.edu/owl/resource/560/01/ http://www.library.cornell.edu/newhelp/res_strategy/citing/apa.htm http://linguistics.byu.edu/faculty/henrichsenl/apa/apa01.html
Related materials	These include any *relevant* material supporting your proposal and/or justifying your argument for doing this research. Include in this section letters from corroborating institutions and or organisations that will provide access to the field of research, people, materials etc.

Please check with your supervisor or your institute as to whether there are any other (specific) requirements you have to take into consideration. Make sure you are aware of the timetable and deadlines. Some final down-to-earth advice: please start writing the proposal as soon as you can. It is in the process of writing that the actual 'structure' will appear – not when you are just thinking about it.

8.3   A Summary in the Form of Questions

In this second paragraph we assume that you have written a proposal and have started executing the research. We will bring to the fore a number of questions that will facilitate the structure and logic of your research. Our assumption here is that most research only really starts to become scholarly when you are in the actual process of execution. The first three questions centre on the research question. The first two not only look at the nature of the question, but also at researcher's attitude, an important factor when conducting research. The third question aims at the context of the research question and researcher.

Question 1: What is the nature of the question? Chap. 1
- What is the problem, who has the problem, who decides whether it actually is a problem?
- Is the presented problem actually the problem – or is there another 'hidden' problem?
- Is the question 'open' or 'closed'?
 The question's nature is 'directive' in the course of research.

Question 2: What is the researcher's basic attitude? Chap. 2
- Research approach ('open' versus 'closed' like searching versus testing).
- Examine as an outsider (keep your distance).
- Engage in conversation with your subject(s) of research (interfere – disturb – intervene).
- Through whose eyes are you going to 'observe' and why?
- How – and in which steps – are you going to 'observe' and why?
- What data will it produce? Are you aware of the different kind of data you might use or generate?
- How are you going to interpret this data? Any specific techniques in mind?
- Check whether the answers on these four questions fit. Are they consistent, logical, do they make sense?

Question 3: Which role does the context play? Chaps. 1 and 2
- What is the context in which the question occurs?
- How important is the context for the research you have in mind?
- Are there specific elements or conditions in the context you should take into consideration?
- Is the context static or dynamic? Assuming that it will probably be dynamic, how are you going to keep track of the developments that might have an impact on your research?

In each research project, theory plays an essential role. Without theory we cannot see what is happening. However, there are distinct differences between research with a closed question and research with an open question. Nevertheless, in both approaches theory serves to clarify how the researcher perceives and describes the reality being examined. This is expressed in the fourth question.

Question 4: What is the role of theory? Chap. 3
- Clarification of notions and assumptions.
- How are these notions specified, in terms of 'sensitising concepts', or are they being operationalised in measurable entities?
- Will you develop a conceptual model and use that model as a framework to elaborate your design?

- Is the focus on knowledge development or a kind of change, be it radical or incremental?
- Are instruments being developed and for what purpose are they being developed?
- How are these instruments applied? Do you have a specific purpose in mind?

The following three questions (five to eight) concern the results of research. At the start of research it can also be advantageous to realise what kind of results are possible and who will or will not benefit from it.

Question 5: What should be the result of this research? Chaps. 4 and 5, Interlude I

- A (tested?) conceptual model?
- A theoretical framework?
- A (mini) theory?
- Instruments?

Question 6: What will (probably) be the purpose of the results of this research? Chap. 7

- There is no purpose.
- New research.
- Improve the current situation.
- Change.
- (Re)design.

Question 7: Who will use the results? Chaps. 1 and 7

- An external client.
- The people in the organisation where the research was conducted.
- Third parties (e.g., external advisors).
- What will be the requirements of the results that the user (or users) will put forward?

Question 8–11 focus on the data. How will the data be collected and analysed, and who will be involved in the analysis?

Question 8: Which data sources will be used in this research? Chaps. 4 and 5

- The (qualitative) data will contain different 'stories' about the perceived 'reality' (or 'realities').
- Nature of data sources: linguistic, visual, numerical.
- Multi-method (observation, interview, literature).

Question 9: How will the analysis of data sources take place? Chaps. 4 and 5
- Interpretation in advance or afterwards.
- Unit of analyse with regard to of sentences (whole-parts-whole).
- Revise and/or analyse data sources: partly quantitative (counting) and partly qualitative (interpretation).
- Comparing different forms of data and/or comparing the same kind of data (across time, across different situations).

Question 10: Who is (primarily) responsible for the interpretation of data? Chap. 6
- Allocating meaning (interpretation) – by the researcher, other actors and 'outsiders'.
- Consensus (group process).
- By means of which hypotheses (whose?).
- By means of a hermeneutical cycle (process method).

Question 11: How will the interpretation of data be arranged? Chaps. 4, 5 and 6
- In a standardised way?
- In advance (or) afterwards?
- Who will participate and why?

Assessing research is often complicated. Questions 12–16 draw the researcher's attention to several important aspects. The appraisal criteria for research depend on whether it is an open or closed question. The criteria for the way in which people are involved in the research may possibly play an important role.

Question 12: Which criteria play a role in the justification of this interpretation? Chap. 6
- Open/closed question: different criteria.
- Criteria that may possibly alter.

Question 13: To whom will you have to give reasons for the design and realisation of the research? Chaps. 1 and 8
- Those involved in the research.
- Problem owners, holders, sponsors.

Question 14: What is the nature of the justification with regard to the design and realisation of the research? Chap. 7
- Process reconstruction and choices (explanation of research actions).
- Explaining the applied 'theoretical view'.
- Personal preference of the researcher (private passion).

Question 15: Which criteria play an (important) part in the justification? Chaps. 6 and 7

- Action repertoire.
- Action plan.

Question 16: How will the testing of criteria take place? Chap. 6

- Based on the 'context of discovery' (actors).
- Based on hypotheses.
- Based on (data) sources.
- Confronting alternative realities (inductive and deductive).
- Triangulation (different data sources, different researchers).
- Testing against literature.
- Representative.

8.4 Checklist for Assessing a Master Thesis or Dissertation

In addition to the previous paragraphs in which the methodological justification of the research design has been discussed through questions – this paragraph provides a brief checklist that can be employed when assessing a complete thesis or dissertation project.

8.4.1 Title and Structure

1. Does the thesis contain a clear, appealing title and an abbreviated subtitle that reflects the essence of the content in one short sentence?
2. Does the book cover bear the name of the author(s) and – if relevant – the name of the client together with other necessary information (education, period covered, status etc.)?
3. Does the thesis start with a preface (this is not the same as a summary!) in which the author(s) informs the reader, for instance, about the reasons for the project and the people who have assisted etc.?
4. Does the thesis contain a well-structured index? In other words, is the reader able to comprehend immediately what the thesis is about by scanning the various titles of the chapters?
5. Does the index contain a logical category in paragraphs so that it is clear how each chapter is composed?
6. Does the index inform the reader where the (literature) references are placed and (if relevant) if there is a thesaurus, index and information about the author?

7. Does the index explain if there are any appendices attached to the thesis and – if so – where these can be found?
8. Does the thesis contain a summary?

8.4.2 Readability

1. Is the report easy to read? Is it attractive? Do you take the reader into the world of your research?
2. Does the whole fit together in such a way that each sentence and paragraph contributes to the complete report?
3. Does the thesis contain a clearly recognisable conceptual structure; in other words, does the author discuss the various issues within a clear framework?
4. Are the subjects discussed thoroughly and are the arguments well-founded?
5. Does the report contain a clear thread? Is the reader aware of which part he is reading and why is he supposed to read it?
6. Has the author chosen a specific tone (e.g., popular, scientific etc.) or style (e.g., we, I, neuter) and is it applied consistently?
7. Are the headlines of the various chapters, illustrations, tables and other figures used effectively; in other words do they have a clear added value?
8. Are illustrations and tables discussed in the text as well or will the reader need to guess where they belong?

8.4.3 Justification

1. Is it absolutely clear which criteria and requirements were used to justify the conclusions and recommendations?
2. Does the author clarify his own point of view (in a justifiable way)?
3. Is it clear what the client can do with the results of the research?
4. Does the report contain recommendations for further research, and if so, are these relevant?

8.4.4 Maintenance

1. Is the project professionally finished (cover, binding, type page, page numbering etc.)?
2. Are the literature references reported correctly and unambiguously in the reference style that has been agreed on?
3. Is the report written in correct Dutch or English and have typing mistakes been removed?
4. Does the report contain the necessary appendices and are they accessible through the index etc.?

8.5   Epilogue

The 16 questions that have been formulated as a result of the preceding chapters are intended to help the researcher design and carry out research. It is probably clear that these questions will have to be answered over and over again while carrying out the research project. There is no such thing as a research or methodology 'cookbook'. Students doing a research project for the first time may find this complicated. However, you could view this differently. Precisely because there are no standard recipes available you have the exciting opportunity to pursue your own path. The most important precondition is that this path is carefully considered. How to systematically justify these choices has been the subject of this book throughout.

References

Bell, J. (2005). *Doing your research project: a guide for first-time researches in education, health and social science*. Maidenhead: Open University Press.

Hart, C. (1998). *Doing a literature review*. London: Sage Publications.

Sloan Devlin, A. (2006). *Research methods: planning, conducting and presenting research*. London: Thomson Learning.

Stinchcombe, A. L. (2005). *The Logic of social research*. Chicago: The University of Chicago Press.

Stace, R. D. & Griffin, D. (2005). *A complexity perspective on researching organizations: taking experience seriously*. London: Routledge.

Tharenou, P., Donohue, R., & Cooper, B. (2007). *Management research methods*. New York: Cambridge University Press.

Chapter 9
Comparative Glossary

Accuracy A term used in survey research to refer to the match between the target population and the sample. Copyright © 1997–2004 Colorado State University, http://writing.colostate.edu/guides/research/glossary/

Action learning A form of management development, which, in essence, involves learning to learn-by-doing with and from others who are also leaning-to-learn by doing (Revans 1980, p. 288). The process is inductive rather than deductive as managers asked to solve actual organizational problems. It crucially depends upon the group as a vehicle for learning by its members to facilitate progress. Its variants in situations throughout the world are described by Revans (1980), Gill and Johnson (1991, p. 164).

Action research Simultaneously bringing about change in the project situation (the action) while learning from the process of deriving the change (the research) (Greenwood and Levin 1998, p. 68).

Action Research is a term for describing a spectrum of activities that focus on research, planning, theorizing, learning, and development. It describes a continuous process of research and learning in the researchers long-term relationship with a problem (Cunningham 1993, p. 161).

Action research challenges the claims of neutrality and objectivity of traditional social science and seeks full collaborative inquiry by all participants, often to engage in sustained change in organizational, community, or institutional contexts (Marshall and Rossman 1999, p. 5).

Action research is one particularly exciting method that can be adopted when working with case research. Here the researchers take on the role of active consultants and influence a process under study (Gummesson 1991, p. 2).

Action research can be described as a family of research methodologies, which pursue action (or change) and research (or understanding) at the same time. In most of its forms it does this by: (a) using a cyclic or spiral process which alternates between action and critical reflection and (b) in the later cycles, continuously refining methods, data and interpretation in the light of the understanding developed in the earlier cycles. It is thus an emergent process which takes shape as understanding increases; it is an iterative process which converges towards a better understanding of what happens. In most of its forms it is also participative (among other reasons, change is usually easier to achieve when those affected by the change are involved) and qualitative. http://www.scu.edu.au/schools/gcm/ar/arhome.html

There is no single type of action research but broadly it can be defined as an approach in which the action researcher and a client collaborate in the diagnosis of problem and in the development of a solution based on the diagnosis (Bryman and Bell 2003, p. 303).

Analysis The processes by which a phenomenon (e.g. a managerial problem) is conceptualized so that it is separated into its component parts and the interrelationships between those parts, and their contribution to the whole, elucidated (Gill and Johnson 1991, p. 164).

J. Jonker and B. Pennink, *The Essence of Research Methodology*,
DOI 10.1007/978-3-540-71659-4_9, © Springer-Verlag Berlin Heidelberg 2010

The working of thought processes (Schatzman and Strauss 1973, p. 109).

A method of inquiry in which one seeks to assess complex systems of thought by 'analysing' them into simpler elements whose relationships are thereby brought into focus (Blackburn 1996).

Analytic frames Systematic, detailed sketches of ideas (or social theories) that a researcher develops in order to aid the examination of a specific phenomenon. In effect, an analytic frame articulates an idea in a way that makes it useful in research. The process of analytical framing is primarily but not entirely deductive (Ragin 1994, p. 183).

Analytic induction A research methodology concerned with the inductive development and testing of theory (Gill and Johnson 1991, p. 164).

Originally, the term had a very strict meaning and was identified with the search for 'universals' in social life. Universals are properties that are invariant. Today, however, analytic induction is often used to refer to any systematic examination of similarities that seeks to develop concepts or ideas. Rather than seeing analytic induction as a search for universals, a search that is likely to fail, it is better to see it as a research strategy that directs investigators to pay close attention to evidence that challenges of disconfirms whatever images they are developing. As researchers accumulate evidence, they compare incidents or cases that appear to be in the same general category with each other. These comparisons establish similarities and differences among incidents or cases that appear to be in the same general category with each other. These comparisons establish similarities and differences among incidents and thus help to define categories and concepts. Evidence that challenges or refutes images that the researcher is constructing from evidence provides important clues for how to alter concepts or shift categories (Ragin 1994, p. 93).

Analytic induction is an approach to the analysis of data in which the researcher seeks universal explanations of phenomena by pursuing the collection of data until no cases that are inconsistent with a hypothetical explanation (deviant or negative cases) of a phenomenon are found (Bryman and Bell 2003, p. 426).

Applicability How can one determine the extent to which the findings of a particular inquiry have applicability in other contexts or which other subjects (respondents)? Management research has to be in part judged by what impact it has on management practice (Griseri 2002, p. 17). Applied research has a practical problem-solving emphasis although the problem solving process is not always generated by a negative circumstance (Cooper and Schindler 2003, p. 14).

Approach A theoretically sustained vantage point for analyzing a subject matter. An approach is more encompassing (but generally less precise) than a conceptual framework: it determines the sets of concepts, questions and perspectives of an inquiry. An approach may also be seen as a quasi-theory or as a pre-theory, a path to theory (Sartori 1984, p. 73).

Assumptions If you make an assumption, you accept that something is true although you have no real proof to it (Collins Cobuild Dictionary 1987, p. 76). Assumptions are often agreed to by various people who are associated with a problem. These assumptions may be established and reaffirmed over history, rather then being challenged or assessed. Assumptions can be continually challenged by asking the question "why?" (Cunningham 1993, p. 57).

Axiological Relating to the study of the nature of values and value judgment (WordNet Dictionary 2003).

Bias In social research is used primarily to describe aspects of a specific research design that may skew findings in some way. Biased measures don't do a good job of measuring the things they are purported to measure and therefore lack validity; biased samples are not representative of the relevant population or set of cases; and so on (Ragin 1994, p. 183).

Bias is the distortion of responses in one direction (Cooper and Schindler 2003, p. 372).

Case study (general) The researcher explores a single entity or phenomenon bounded by time and activity and collects detailed information by using a variety of data collection procedures during a sustained period of time (Creswell 1994, p. 12).

Reports of research on a specific organization, program, or process are often called case studies (Marshall and Rossman 1999, p. 159).

A case study, by contrast, is, or should be, designed as a learning vehicle with specific educational objectives in mind (Easton 1992, p. 1).

The collection and presentation of detailed information about a particular participant or small group, frequently including the accounts of subjects themselves. Copyright © 1997–2004 Colorado State University, http://writing.colostate.edu/guides/research/glossary/

Case studies place emphasis on a full contextual analysis of fewer events or conditions and their interrelations for a single subject or respondent. Although hypotheses are often used, the reliance on qualitative data makes support or rejection more difficult (Cooper and Schindler 2001, p. 137).

A research design that entails the detailed and intensive analysis of a single case. The term is sometimes extended to include the study of just two or three cases for comparative purposes (Bryman and Bell 2003, p. 53).

Case study (embedded) A case study involves more than one unit of analysis. In a single case also attention is given to a subunit or subunits. These subunits are then referred to as the embedded units (Yin 2003, p. 42, 43).

Category A concept unifying a number of observations have some characteristics in common (Dey 1993, p. 275).

Categories must have two aspects, an internal – they must be meaningful in relation to the data – and an external aspect – they must be meaningful in relation to the other categories (Dey 1993, p. 96).

Causal relationship The relationship established that shows that an independent variable, and nothing else, causes a change in a dependent variable. Establishes, also, how much of a change is shown in the dependent variable. Copyright © 1997–2004 Colorado State University, http://writing.colostate.edu/guides/research/glossary/

Classification A process of organizing data into categories or classes and identifying formal connections between them (Dey 1993, p. 275).

Sartori adds: A classification requires a single criterion which serves as the basis of division. When multiple criteria or dimensions are involved, we have a typology and/or taxonomy (Sartori 1984, p. 73).

Coding Initial indexing, referred to as coding, proceeds by means of the tentative labelling of the phenomena which the knowledge engineer perceives in a specified piece of text and which he or she considers to be of potential relevance to the knowledge domain (Pidgeon 1991, p. 161).

In quantitative research, codes act as tags that are placed on data about people or other units of analysis. The aim is to assign the data relating to each variable to groups, each of which is considered to be a category of the variable in question. Numbers are then assigned to each category to allow the information to be processed by the computer. In qualitative research, coding is the process whereby data are broken down in component parts, which are given names (Bryman and Bell 2003, p. 157).

Assigning numbers or other symbols to answers so that responses can be tallied and grouped into a limited number of classes or categories (Cooper and Schindler 2001, p. 424)

Coding (open) The process of breaking down, examining, comparing, conceptualizing and categorizing data (Strauss and Corbin 1990, p. 61).

This process of coding yields concepts, which are later to be grouped and turned into categories (Bryman and Bell 2003, p. 429).

Coding (axial) A set of procedures whereby data are put back together in new ways after open coding, by making connections between categories. (Strauss and Corbin 1990, p. 96).

This is done by linking codes to contexts, to consequences, to patterns of interaction, and to causes (Bryman and Bell 2003, p. 429).

Coding (selective) The procedure of selecting the core category, systematically relating it to other categories, validating those relationships, and filling in categories that need further refinement and development (Strauss and Corbin 1990, p. 116).

A core category is the central issue or focus around which all other categories are integrated. It is what Strauss and Corbin call the storyline that frames your account (Bryman and Bell 2003, p. 429).

Comparative method The family of techniques employed in comparative political research. (Martin and Shaun 1998, p. 12).

We not only speak of comparing incident to incident to classify them, but we also make use of what we call theoretical comparisons (Strauss and Corbin 1998, p. 78).

Theoretical comparisons are tools (a list of properties) for looking at something somewhat objectively rather than naming or classifying without a thorough examination of the object at the property and dimensional levels (Strauss and Corbin 1998, p. 80).

Concept A concept is an idea or abstract principle, which relates to a particular subject or to a particular view of that subject (Collins Cobuild Dictionary 1987, p. 288).

A concept is a labelled phenomenon. It is an abstract representation of an event, object, or action/interaction that a researcher identifies as being significant in the data (Strauss and Corbin 1998, p. 103).

A concept is used to indicate the meaning of a word, a constituency of thoughts, and a way of thinking about an object (Dictionary of Modern Thought 1977, p. 153).

Abstractions, which allow us to order, out our impressions of the world by enabling us to identify similarities and differences in phenomena and thereby classify them (Gill and Johnson 1991, p. 164).

A concept is simply an abstract way of thinking about a situation. It is a summary of some phenomenon that you have data on (Easton 1992, p. 48).

A general idea which stands for a class of concepts (Dey 1993, p. 275).

A name given to a category that organizes observations and ideas by virtue of their possessing common features (Bryman and Bell 2003, p. 71).

A bundle of meanings or characteristics associated with certain events, objects, conditions, or situations (Cooper and Schindler 2001, p. 39).

Conceptual Conceptual means related to the idea of concepts formed in the mind (Collins Cobuild Dictionary 1987, p. 288).

Conceptual schema If research ultimately shows the concepts and constructs and if the propositions that specify the connections can be supported, the researcher will have the beginning of a conceptual scheme (Cooper and Schindler 2003, p. 45).

Conceptual travelling and stretching The terms reflect the concern in the problem of applying categories across diverse contexts. Conceptual travelling means the application of concepts to new cases. Conceptual stretching reflects the distortion that occurs when a concept does not fit the new cases. Sartori encourages the scholar to be attentive to context, but without abandoning broad comparison (Sartori 1984).

Confirmability Objectivity; the findings of the study could be confirmed by another person conducting the same study. Copyright © 1997–2004 Colorado State University, http://writing. colostate.edu/guides/research/glossary/

Constant comparison Inductive category coding and simultaneous comparing of units of meaning across categories. Constant comparison is the exploration of similarities and differences across incidents in the data. By comparing where the facts are similar of different the researcher can generate concepts and concept properties based on recurring patterns of behaviour.

Consistency How can one determine whether the findings of an inquiry would be repeated if the inquiry were replicated with the same (or similar) subjects (respondents) in the same (of similar) context?

Compatibility or harmony between things, acts or statements (Websters Comprehensive Dictionary 1996, p. 278).

Constructivism The belief that knowledge is made up largely of social interpretations rather than the awareness of an external reality (Stake 1995, p. 170).

Constructivism provides a fruitful theoretical framework for understanding and describing knowledge-use in human activity systems (Cassell and Symon 1994, p. 73).

Constructivism is an ontological position (often also referred to as constructionism) that asserts that social phenomena and their meanings are continually being accomplished by social actors. It implies that social phenomena and categories are not only produced through social interaction but that they are in a constant state of revision (Bryman and Bell 2003, p. 20).

Context The context of something consists of the ideas, situation, events, or information that relate to it and make it possible to understand it fully (Collins Cobuild Dictionary 1987, p. 305).

Control group In experimentation, a group of subjects to whom no experimental stimulus is administrate and who should resemble the experimental group in all other respects. The comparison of the *control group* and the experimental group at the end of the experiment points to the effect of the experimental stimulus (Babbie 1998).

Co-operative Inquiry Can be seen as "cycling through" the phases of reflection and action.

Agreement on focus of inquiry and develop together a set of questions or propositions (propositional knowing).

Co-researchers and co-objects engage in action and observe and record the process and outcomes of their own and each other's experience (practical knowing).

The touchstone of the approach is that any practical skills or theoretical propositions, which emerge, can be said to derive from and be congruent with this experience.

Co-operative inquiry is an inquiry strategy in which all those involved in the research endeavour are both co-researchers, whose thinking and decision-making contributes to generating ideas, designing and managing the project, and drawing conclusions from the experience; and *also* co-subjects, participating in the activity which is being researched.

Co-operative inquiry is a way of working with other people who have similar concerns and interests to your self, in order to:

(a) Understand your world, make sense of your life and develop new and creative ways of looking at things;

(b) Learn how to act to change things you may want to change and find out how to do things better.

Co-operative Inquiry is a systematic approach to developing understanding and action (Reason 1999, p. 207).

Credibility A researcher's ability to demonstrate that the object of a study is accurately identified and described based on the way in which the study was conducted. Copyright © 1997–2004 Colorado State University, http://writing.colostate.edu/guides/research/glossary/

Critical case The idea here is that if a proposition can be shown to work when conditions are least favourable for its validity, it is likely to be valid in all other circumstances as well. If democracies are now consolidating in countries, which have no previous experience of that form of rule, we can be sure that the modern move toward democracy is significant. Alternatively, a proposition, which fails to work even in the most favourable conditions, can quickly be dismissed. If post-material values are nowhere to be found among graduates in the wealthiest countries, then the theory of post-materialism is no good. Depending on expectations, we can set out either to support a theory by showing its value in unfavourable conditions (a 'least favourable' design) or to disprove a theory be showing it fails even in favourable circumstances (a most favourable design) (Hague et al. 1998).

Data (analysis) Processing observations to draw out their meanings (Stake 1995, p. 170).

Editing and reducing accumulated data to a manageable size, developing summaries, looking for patterns, and applying statistical techniques (Cooper and Schindler 2001, p. 82).

We define data analysis as consisting of three concurrent flows of activity: data reduction, data display, and conclusion drawing/verification. The analysis is a continuous, iterative enterprise.

Data reduction refers to the process of selecting, simplifying, abstracting, and transforming the data that appear in written-up field notes or transcriptions.

A data display is an organized, compressed assembly of information that permits conclusion drawing and action (Miles and Huberman 1994, p. 10).

Data (collection) The finding and gathering (or generating) of materials that the researcher will then analyse (Straus 1987, p. 20).

Data (general) Data is information, usually in the form of facts or statistics that you can analyse, or that you can use to do further calculation (Collins Cobuild Dictionary 1987, p. 357).

Recorded observations, usually in numeric or textual form. Copyright © 1997–2004 Colorado State University, http://writing.colostate.edu/guides/research/glossary/

Facts (attitudes, behaviour, motivations, etc.) collected from respondents or observations (mechanical or direct) plus published information; categorized as primary and secondary (Cooper and Schindler 2001, p. 82).

Data (Qualitative) Data, which deals with numbers rather than meanings (Dey 1993, p. 276). This data is often referred to as being rich, since it captures the richness of detail and nuance of the phenomena being studied (Hussey and Hussey 1997, p. 56).

Data (nature) Data can be classified based on its nature. A distinction can be made between *linguistic data* (e.g. transcription of a conversation), *numerical* (in figures) *data* (e.g. a company's profit and loss account) and *visual data* (e.g. drawings, pictures, photos, rich pictures etc.).

Deconstruction It is a method of conducting an internal critique of texts. In essence, a deconstructive approach of textual analysis aims at exposing what is concealed within or has left out of a text (Hesse-Biber and Leavy 2006, p. 292).

Ideas need to be understood in historical context, and hence is bound to social practice. There are unarticulated foundations of ideas in every historical context.

Deduction The deduction of particular instances from general inferences, it entails the development of a conceptual and theoretical structure, which is then tested by observation (Gill and Johnson 1991, p. 164).

The process of driving more specific ideas or propositions from general ideas, knowledge, or theories and working out their implications for a specific set of evidence or specific kinds of evidence (Ragin 1994, p. 186).

The forming of conclusions by applying the rules of logic to a premise (Encarta 2004).

An approach to the relationship between theory and research in which the latter is conducted with reference to hypotheses and ideas inferred from the former (Bryman and Bell 2003, p. 10).

A form of inference in which the conclusion must necessarily follow from the reasons given; a deduction is valid if it is impossible for the conclusion to be false if the premises are true (Cooper and Schindler 2001, p. 34).

Deductive Is used to describe a method of reasoning where conclusions are deduced logically from other things that are already known (Collins Cobuild Dictionary 1987, p. 366).

Based on logical or reasonable deduction (Encarta World English Dictionary 2004).

A form of reasoning in which conclusions are formulated about particulars from general or universal premises. Copyright © 1997–2004 Colorado State University, http://writing.colostate. edu/guides/research/glossary/

Dependability Being able to account for changes in the design of the study and the changing conditions surrounding what was studied. Copyright © 1997–2004 Colorado State University, http://writing.colostate.edu/guides/research/glossary/

Dependent variable The aspect or attribute of cases or observations that the investigators hope to explain or in some way account for (Ragin 1994, p. 186).

The phenomenon whose variation the researcher is trying to explain or understand (Gill and Johnson 2002, p. 226).

Descriptive statistics Statistical computations describing either the characteristics of a sample or the relationship among variables in a sample. It merely summarizes a set of sample observations, whereas inferential statistics move beyond the description of a specific observation to make inferences about the larger population from which the sample observations were drawn (Babbie 1998, p. G2).

Design flexibility A quality of an observational study that allows researchers to pursue inquiries on new topics or questions that emerges from initial research. Copyright © 1997–2004 Colorado State University, http://writing.colostate.edu/guides/research/glossary/

Dichotomous variable A variable having only two categories. Also called binomial and/or binary variable (Babbie 1998).

A variable said to have only two values: the presence or absence of a property/construct (Cooper and Schindler 2003, p. 47).

Discourse community A community of scholars and researchers in a given field who respond to and communicate to each other through published articles in the community's journals and presentations at conventions. All members of the discourse community adhere to certain conventions for the presentation of their theories and research. Copyright © 1997–2004 Colorado State University, http://writing.colostate.edu/guides/research/glossary/

Display Something intended to communicate a particular impression (WordNet 2003).

Emic A form of explanation of its situation or events that relies upon elucidation of actor's internal logics or subjectivity (Gill and Johnson 1991, p. 164).

The research strategy that focuses on local explanations and criteria of significance (Kottak 2004, p. 338).

Empirical Knowledge, study, relies on practical experience rather than theories. Collins Cobuild Dictionary (1987, p. 462).

Points to testing subjective beliefs against objective reality (Cooper and Schindler 2003, p. 13).

If a scientist believes something is so, he must somehow or other put his belief to a test outside himself. Subjective believe, in other words, must be checked against objective reality (Kerlinger 1973, p. 11).

Empiricism The idea that valid knowledge is directly derived from sense data and experience (Gill and Johnson 1991, p. 165).

An approach to the study of reality that suggests that only knowledge gained through experience and the senses is acceptable (Bryman and Bell 2003, p. 9).

Observations and propositions based on sense experience and/or derived from such experience by methods of inductive logic, including mathematics and statistics (Cooper and Schindler 2001, p. 31).

Epistemology The philosophical theory of knowledge, which seeks to define it, distinguishes its principal varieties, identify its sources, and establish its limits (Dictionary of Modern Thought 1977, p. 279).

The branch of philosophy concerned with the study of the criteria by which we determine what does and does not constitute warranted or valid knowledge (Gill and Johnson 1991, p. 165).

That department of philosophy, which investigates critically the nature, grounds, limits, and criteria, or validity of human knowledge (Webster's Comprehensive Dictionary 1996, p. 428).

An epistemological issue concerns the question of what is (or should be) regarded as acceptable knowledge in a discipline (Bryman and Bell 2003, p. 13).

The branch of philosophy concerned with the study of the criteria by which we determine (i.e. know) what does and does not constitute warranted or valid knowledge (Gill and Johnson 2002, p. 226).

Ethnography In which the researcher studies an intact cultural group in a natural setting during a prolonged period of time collecting, primarily, observational data. The research process is flexible and typically evolves contextually in response to the lived realities encountered in the field settings (Creswell 1994, p. 11).

Ethnography is both a product, a concrete text occurring within a genre of writing, and a process of gathering and thinking about data in relation to certain issues (Dictionary of Modern Thought 1977, p. 286).

Ethnography is the branch of anthropology in which different cultures are studied and described (Collins Cobuild Dictionary 1987, p. 480).

Like participant observation, a research method in which the researcher immerses him- or herself in a social setting for an extended period of time, observing behaviour, listening to what is said in conversations both between others and with the fieldworker, and asking questions. However, the term has a more inclusive sense than participant observation, which seems to emphasize the observational component. Also, the term 'an ethnography' is frequently used to refer to the written output of ethnographic research (Bryman and Bell 2003, p. 316).

Ethno-methodology A form of ethnography that studies activities of group members to see how they make sense of their surroundings. Copyright © 1997–2004 Colorado State University, http:// writing.colostate.edu/guides/research/glossary/

Ethno-methodology draws on the phenomenological perspective and is related to phenomenology in that both focus on the process whereby individuals understand and give sense of order to the world in which they live. Ethno-methodology was popularized as a perspective in the field of sociology in the 1960s through the work of Harold Garfinkel (1967), Hess-Biber and Leavy (2006, p. 35).

Experiment The manipulation of natural phenomena to answer practical or theoretical questions (Dictionary of Modern Thought 1977, p. 299).

An experiment is a scientific test which done in order to prove that a theory is true or to discover what happens to something in particular conditions (Collins Cobuild Dictionary 1987, p. 494).

A research design that rules out alternative explanations of findings deriving from it (i.e. possesses internal validity) by having at least (a) an experimental group, which is exposed to a treatment, and a control group, which is not, and (b) random assignment to the two groups (Bryman and Bell 2003, p. 39).

Explanatory research It is a study that goes beyond description and attempt to explain the reasons for the phenomenon. In an explanatory study, the researcher uses theories or at least hypothesis to account for the forces that caused a certain phenomenon to occur (Cooper and Schindler 2003, p. 11).

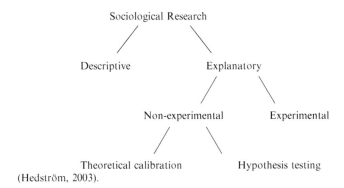

(Hedström, 2003).

Explanatory studies Attempts to explain the reasons for the phenomenon that the descriptive study only observed; answers why (Cooper and Schindler 2001, p. 13).

External invalidity Refers to the possibility that conclusions drawn from experimental results may not be generalizable to the 'real' world (Babbie 1998).

External validity External validity is concerned with the interaction of the experimental treatment with other factors and the resulting impact on the ability to generalize to (and across) times, settings, or persons (Cooper and Schindler 2003, p. 434).

Falsification In this fashion, theoretical development is an ongoing process in which the creators of a theory keep working to test their creation in order to destroy it and replace it with something better. (Gummesson 1991, p. 80).

Focused comparisons Comparisons that concentrate on intensive study of an aspects of the cases in a small number of cases (two-to-four cases). Comparative Methods Dictionary http://poli.haifa.ac.il/~levi/dictionary.html

Functionalism A paradigm that focuses on the functions served by the elements making up a whole system or organism. Thus, one of the functions of higher education is to keep young people out of the job market (Babbie 1998).

Functional equivalence The notion of functional equivalence descends from the idea that every political system necessarily fulfils certain fundamental tasks. The same tasks may be performed however by different structures while the same structures may fulfil, in different countries, different tasks. Two institutions or processes are functionally equivalent when they fulfil the same role within the political system. Institutions with the same function not necessarily perform exactly the same functions; monarchs my rule with a rod of iron or just dispense medals to worthy citizens. Also, difference processes can perform the same function; For example, elections and revolutions are devices for repealing the governing elite (Dogan and Pelassy 1984, pp. 5–6; Hague et al. 1998, p. 274).

Generalisability What is the probability that patters observed in a sample will also be present in the wider population from which the sample is drawn?

How likely is it that ideas and theories generated in one setting will also apply in other settings?

The extent to which research findings and conclusions from a study conducted on a sample population can be applied to the population at large. Copyright © 1997–2004 Colorado State University, http://writing.colostate.edu/guides/research/glossary/

That quality of a research finding that justifies the inference that it represents something more than the specific observations on which it was based. If you discover why people commit burglaries, can you *generalize* that discovery to other crimes as well? (Babbie 1998)

The ability to draw inferences and conclusions from data (Salkind 2000, p. 86).

A concern with the external validity of research findings (Bryman and Bell 2003, p. 81).

Grounded theory Theory that was derived from data systematically gathered and analyzed through the research process. In this method, data collection, analysis, and eventual theory stand in close relationship to one another (Strauss and Corbin 1998, p. 12).

The researcher attempts to derive a theory by using multiple stages of data collection and the refinement and interrelationship of categories of information (Creswell 1994, p. 12).

Grounded Theory is a general methodology for developing theory that is grounded in data systematically gathered and analyzed (Denzin and Lincoln 1994, p. 204).

The outcome of inductive research, that is, theory created or discovered through the observation of particular cases (Gill and Johnson 1991, p. 165).

Practice of developing other theories that emerge from observing a group. Theories are grounded in the group's observable experiences, but researchers add their own insight into why those experiences exist. Copyright © 1997–2004 Colorado State University, http://writing. colostate.edu/guides/research/glossary/

An approach to the analysis of qualitative data that aims to generate theory out of research data by achieving a close fit between the two (Bryman and Bell 2003, p. 428).

Hermeneutic circle The notion that no observation or description is free from the observer's interpretation based upon his or her presuppositions and projection of his or her values, theories, etc. on to phenomena (Gill and Johnson 1991, p. 165).

Hermeneutics Hermeneutics is based on the ontological position that the world is objectively given; the epistemological project is to make interpretations of this subjective world (Greenwood and Levin 1998, p. 68).

The art, skill or theory of interpretation, of understanding the significance of human actions, utterances, products and institutions (Dictionary of Modern Thought 1977, p. 389).

An approach to the analysis of texts that stresses how prior understanding and prejudices shape the interpretive process (Denzin and Lincoln 1994, p. 15).

Hermeneutics is concerned with interpreting and understanding the products of the human mind, which characterize the social and cultural world (Burrel and Morgan 1979, p. 235).

A discipline concerned with the interpretation of literary texts and/or meaningful human behaviour (Gill and Johnson 1991, p. 165).

A term drawn from theology, which, when imported into the social sciences, is concerned with the theory and method of the interpretation of human action. It emphasizes the need to understand from the perspective of the social actor (Bryman and Bell 2003, p. 421).

Holistic perspective Taking almost every action or communication of the whole phenomenon of a certain community or culture into account in research. Copyright © 1997–2004 Colorado State University, http://writing.colostate.edu/guides/research/glossary/

A perspective on the practice of qualitative research in that it is reflexive and process-driven, ultimately producing culturally situated and theory-enmeshed knowledge through an ongoing interplay between theory and methods, researcher and researched (Hesse-Biber and Leavy 2006, p. 36).

Hypotheses A tentative proposal that explains and predicts the variation in a particular phenomenon (Gill and Johnson 1991, p. 165).

A tentative explanation based on theory to predict a causal relationship between variables. Copyright © 1997–2004 Colorado State University, http://writing.colostate.edu/guides/research/ glossary/

A specific proposition or 'educated guesses' regarding what researchers expect to find in a body of evidence, based on their substantive and theoretical knowledge. In standard applications of the scientific method, hypotheses are tested with data specifically collected for the hypotheses (Ragin 1994, p. 187).

A theoretical explanation of the behaviour of phenomena that can be tested against the facts. A hypothesis can be refuted, unlike a tautology, which is true by definition, but it may not be possible to prove that it is correct. Comparative Methods Dictionary, http://poli.haifa.ac.il/~levi/dictionary.html

A proposition formulated for empirical testing; a tentative or conjectural declarative belief or statement that describes the relationship between two or more variables (Cooper and Schindler 2001, p. 47).

An educated guess to be tested (Salkind 2000, p. 25).

An informed speculation, which is set up to be tested, about the possible relationship between two or more variables (Bryman and Bell 2003, p. 9).

A conjectural statement of the relation between two or more variables. Hypotheses are always in declarative sentence form, and the related, either generally or specifically, variables to variables.

If a scientist believes something is so, he must somehow or other put his belief to a test outside himself. Subjective believe, in other words, must be checked against objective reality (Kerlinger 1973, p. 18).

Ideal types 1. An ideal type is an analytical construct that serves as a measuring rod for social observers to determine the extent to which concrete social institutions are similar and how they differ from some defined measure. The ideal type involves determining the 'logically consistent' features of a social institution. The ideal type never corresponds to concrete reality but is a description to which we can compare reality. 'Ideal Capitalism,' for example, is used extensively in social science literature. According to the ideal type, capitalism consists of four basic features: Private Ownership; Pursuit of Profit; Competition; *Laissez Faire*. In reality, all capitalist systems deviate from the theoretical construct we call 'ideal capitalism.' But the construct allows us to compare and contrast economic systems of various societies to this definition (Sartori 1984, p. 78).

2. In order to conceptualized and generalized historical events and processes despite their uniqueness, Max Weber, suggested the construction of 'ideal type': concepts that are constructed by the researchers (and thus are not 'real') and capture the basic characteristics of a series of cases. This abstract construct is called 'ideal type'. And Sartori adds: ideal types are heuristic construct that does not reflect frequency or probability of empirical occurrence. When construed as a polar end of a continuum or of a serial order, it coincides with a polar concept. When construed as a parameter or model (archetype) an ideal type is also called 'pure type'. Max Weber Home-Page; Comparative Methods Dictionary, http://poli.haifa.ac.il/~levi/dictionary.html

Ideographic An approach to social science that emphasizes that explanation of human behaviour is possible only through gaining access to actors' subjectivity or culture (Gill and Johnson 1991, p. 165).

Independent variable Are also known as causal variables. When one variable is used to explain or account for the variation in another variable, it is called causal or independent. Variation in levels of nutrition, for example, may be used as an independent variable to account for variation in average life expectancy across countries (Ragin 1994, p. 188).

A variable from which the values of other variables are derived. Comparative Methods Dictionary, http://poli.haifa.ac.il/~levi/dictionary.html

Indexicality The problem that people vary their behaviour according to their interpretation of the situation in which they find themselves (Gill and Johnson 1991, p. 165).

Indicator   An observation that we choose to consider as a reflection of a variable we wish to study. Thus for example, attending church might be considered an *indicator* of religiosity (Babbie 1998, p. G3). Used within the idea of the three-level character of concepts. Concepts can be measured by first defining the concept itself, second by finding dimensions of the concept and third finding indicators on the empirical level that are related to the dimensions (Goertz 2006, p. 6).

Induction   General inferences induced from particular instances, or the development of theory from the observation of empirical reality (Gill and Johnson 1991, p. 188).

   The process of using evidence to formulate or reformulate a general idea. Generally, whenever evidence is used as a basis for generating concepts, as in qualitative research, or empirical generalizations, as in quantitative research, induction has played a part (Ragin 1994, p. 188).

   To draw a conclusion from one of more particular facts or pieces of evidence; the conclusion explains the facts (Cooper and Schindler 2001, p. 35).

Inductive   A form of reasoning in which a generalized conclusion is formulated from particular instances. Copyright © 1997–2004 Colorado State University, http://writing.colostate.edu/guides/research/glossary/

   Relating to the process of deriving general principles from particular facts or instances (The American Heritage: dictionary 2000).

   An approach to the relationship between theory and research in which the former is generated out of the latter (Bryman and Bell 2003, p. 280).

Inductive analysis   A form of analysis based on inductive reasoning; a researcher using inductive analysis starts with answers, but forms questions throughout the research process. Copyright © 1997–2004 Colorado State University, http://writing.colostate.edu/guides/research/glossary/

Inference   Is the process of using the facts we know to learn about facts we do not know. The facts we do not know are the subjects of our research questions, theories, and hypotheses. The facts we do know form our (quantitative or qualitative) data or observations. (King et al. 1994, p. 46). Comparative Methods Dictionary, http://poli.haifa.ac.il/~levi/dictionary.html

Interpretation   The interpretation of a particular situation, law, statement is the explanation of what it means (Collins Cobuild Dictionary 1987, p. 763).

   To interpret is to make action meaningful to others, not just or even necessarily within the terms used by the actors themselves (Dey 1993, p. 39).

   A technical term used in connection with the elaboration model. It represents the research outcome in which a control variable is discovered to be the mediating factor through which an independent variable has its effect on a dependent variable. (Babbie 1998).

Inquiry (narrative)   A qualitative research approach based on a researcher's narrative account of the investigation, not to be confused with a narrative examined by the researcher as data. Copyright © 1997–2004 Colorado State University, http://writing.colostate.edu/guides/research/glossary/

Inquiry (naturalistic)   Observational research of a group in its natural setting. Copyright © 1997–2004 Colorado State University, http://writing.colostate.edu/guides/research/glossary/

Inquiry (rhetorical)   'entails...(1) identifying a motivational concern, (2) posing questions, (3) engaging in a heuristic search (which in composition studies has often occurred by probing other fields), (4) creating a new theory or hypotheses, and (5) justifying the theory' (Lauer and Asher 1988, p. 5), Copyright © 1997–2004 Colorado State University, http://writing.colostate.edu/guides/research/glossary/

Invalidity (external)   Refers to the possibility that conclusions drawn from experimental results may not be generalizable to the 'real' World (Babbie 1998).

Invalidity (internal) Refers to the possibility that the conclusions drawn from experimental results may not accurately reflect what went on in the experiment itself (Babbie 1998).

Knowledge (experiential) Experiential knowledge may be traditional or modern. It is frequently specific to a local context and is acquired through individual and collective learning. Experiential knowledge has often not been systematically validated or tested but is nevertheless dynamic and is used by all of us in our daily lives. Such knowledge must not be confused with pseudo-science, which is largely static – changing only in opposition to systematic science – and has no societal benefit. ISCU report (2004).

Knowledge (explicit) Knowledge that can be expressed formally using a system of symbols, and can therefore be easily communicated or diffused (Choo 1998, p. 112).

Explicit knowledge is codifiable, objective, impersonal, context independent and easy to share. Explicit knowledge is regarded objective, standing above and separate from both individual and social value systems (Hisloop 2005, p. 19).

Knowledge (practical) The practice-based nature of knowledge assumes that knowledge develops through practice: people's knowledge develops as they conduct activities and gain expertise. Knowledge involves the active agency of people making decisions in light of the specific circumstances in which they find themselves (Hisloop 2005, p. 31).

Knowledge gained through habit and intuition (Baumard 1999, p. 63).

Knowledge (tacit) Tacit knowledge is inexpressible in a codifiable form, subjective, personal, context specific and difficult to share. Tacit knowledge represents knowledge that people possess, but which is inexpressible (Hislop 2005, p. 19).

Something we know but cannot express (Baumard 1999, p. 2).

The implicit knowledge used by organizational members to perform their work and to make sense of their worlds. It is knowledge that is un-codified and difficult to diffuse (Choo 1998, p. 111).

'Know how' or intelligence (Jashapara 2004, p. 17).

Meaning The meaning of a world, expression, or gesture is the thing or idea that it refers to or represents and which can be explained using other words (Collins Cobuild Dictionary 1987, p. 900).

The customary significance attached to the use of a word, phrase, or sentence, including both its literal sense and its emotive associations; what is elucidated in a definition. www. philosophypages.com

There are three specific ways of interpreting meaning: meaning = significance (importance); meaning = purpose (orientation); meaning = understanding (content) (Arbnor and Bjerke 1997, p. 33).

Measure (nominal) A level of measurement describing a variable the different attributes of which are only different, as distinguished from ordinal, interval, or ratio measures. Gender would be an example of nominal measure (Babbie 1998).

Measurement Measurement is the activity or process of measuring something (Collins Cobuild Dictionary 1987, p. 901).

Assigning numbers to empirical events in compliance with a mapping rule (Cooper and Schindler 2001, p. 203).

Assigning of values to objects, events or outcomes according to rules (Salkind 2000, p. 100).

Measures Implementations of variables in a particular set of data. Generally every variable may be measured in a variety of ways, and researchers must justify the specific measures they use for each variable (Ragin 1994, p. 189).

Memos The researchers record of analysis, thoughts, interpretations, questions, and directions for further data collection (Strauss and Corbin 1987, p. 110).

Writing, in which the researcher puts down theoretical questions, hypotheses, summary of codes, etc. A method of keeping track of coding results and stimulating further coding, and also a major means for integrating the theory (Strauss 1987, p. 22).

Methodological individualism A methodological approach that holds that all description and explanation of social phenomena should ultimately be in terms of individuals, their properties and their interrelations in terms of their properties. And in a similar formulation: The elementary unit of social life is the individual human action. To explain social institutions and social change is to show how they arise as the result of the action and interaction of individuals (Elstar 1989, p. 13; Franssen 1997, p. 10).

Methodology (general) An explicit way of structuring one's thinking and actions in terms of research.

A way of thinking about and studying social reality (Strauss and Corbin 1998, p. 3).

The study or description of the method or procedures used in some activity (Dictionary of Modern Thought 1977, p. 525).

The study of the methods or procedures used in a discipline so as to gain warranted knowledge (Gill and Johnson 1991, p. 165).

Methodology (qualitative) It is the theoretical perspective into the social world. It is a way of thinking about and studying social reality (Straus and Corbin 1998, p. 3).

Methodology (quantitative) An explicit way of structuring one's thinking and actions (Jayaratna 1994, p. 37).

Methods A set of procedures and techniques for gathering and analysing data (Strauss and Corbin 1998, p. 3).

A particular way of doing something (Collins Cobuild Dictionary 1987, p. 910).

Mental models A group or network of interrelated concepts that reflect conscious or subconscious perceptions of reality. These internal mental networks of meaning are constructed as people draw inferences and gather information about the world. Copyright © 1997–2004 Colorado State University, http://writing.colostate.edu/guides/research/glossary/

Minimal definition A definition that includes the defining properties (or characteristics) and excludes the accompanying properties (Sartori 1984, p. 79).

Model A representation of something else, designed for a special purpose. This representation may take many forms, depending upon the purpose in hand (Dictionary of Modern Thought 1977, p. 536).

A model is not a causal network but is more like a chain of events. It is a strategy of developing linkages between concepts, nothing regularities arousing one's curiosity (Cunningham 1993, p. 161).

A drastically simplified representation of the real world endowed with strong explanatory power. Comparative Methods Dictionary, http://poli.haifa.ac.il/~levi/dictionary.html

An exemplary, paradigmatic, idealized case (Sartori 1984, p. 79).

A representation of a system that is constructed to study some aspect of that system or the system as a whole (Cooper and Schindler 2001, p. 52).

An intellectual construct, descriptive of an entity in which at least one observer has an interest. The observer may wish to relate his model and, if appropriate, its mechanisms, to observables in the world. When this is done it frequently leads – understandable, but not accurately – to descriptions of the world couched in terms of models, as if the world were identical with models of it (Checkland 1999, p. 315).

Multi-method research May often be used synonymously with triangulation, as multiple measurements are perhaps the multi-method strategy's most familiar application. However, with Brewer and Hunter (1989) we use the term multi-method research more widely, to include its application to all phases of the management research process (Gill and Johnson 1991, p. 165).

Employing different types of methods to help to guard against and to correct for inherent methodological biases either for or against certain types of theories (Brewer and Hunter 1989, p. 53).

Naturalism According to the positivist school of thought, social phenomena could be researched in a similar way as natural sciences.

Any philosophy, which sees, mind as dependent upon, included within, or emergent from material nature, and not as being prior to or in some way more real than it (Dictionary of Modern Thought 1977, p. 565).

The necessity to investigate human action in its natural or everyday setting and that the researcher must avoid disturbing that setting (Gill and Johnson 1991, p. 165).

A confusing term that has at least three distinct meanings; a commitment to adopting the principles of natural scientific method; being true to the nature of the phenomenon being investigated; and a style of research that seeks to minimize the intrusion of artificial methods of data collection (Bryman and Bell 2003, p. 36).

Neutrality How can one establish the degree to which the findings of an inquiry are determined by the subjects (respondents) and conditions of the inquiry and not by the biases, motivation, interests, or perspectives of the inquirer?

Nomothetic An approach to explanation in which we seek to identify a few causal factors that generally impact class of conditions or events. Imagine the two or three key factors that determine which college's students choose, such as proximity, reputation, and so forth (Babbie 1998).

Approaches to social science that seek to construct a deductively tested set of general theories that explain and predict human behaviour. It emphasizes on the importance of basing research upon systematic protocol and technique (Gill and Johnson 2002, p. 44, 228).

Normative statements Statement that is neither factual nor hypothetical (Sartori 1984, p. 79).

Null hypothesis Hypothesis that suggests there is no relationship among the variables under study. You may conclude that the variables are related after having statistically rejected the null hypothesis (Babbie 1998).

This hypothesis is a statement that no difference exists between the parameter (a measure taken by a census of the population or a prior measurement of a sample of the population) and the statistic being compared to it (a measure from a recently drawn sample of the population). A null hypothesis is used for testing (Cooper and Schindler 2003, p. 523).

Observation Observation is the process of carefully watching someone or something, especially in order to learn or understand something about him (Collins Cobuild Dictionary 1987, p. 991).

The full range of monitoring behavioural and non-behavioural activities and conditions (including record analysis, physical condition analysis, physical process analysis, nonverbal analysis, linguistic analysis, extra linguistic analysis and spatial analysis) (Cooper and Schindler 2001, p. 371).

Ontology The theory of existence or, more narrowly, of what really exists, as opposed to that which appears to exist, but does not, or to that which can properly be said to exist but only if conceived as some complex whose constituents are the things that really exist (Dictionary of Modern Thought 1977, p. 608).

The study of the essence of phenomena and the nature of their existence (Gill and Johnson 1991, p. 165).

A theory of the nature of social entities (Bryman and Bell 2003, p. 19).

Ontology (philosophy) Relates to our assumptions of reality such as whether it is external or a construct of our minds (Jaspahara 2004, p. 93).

Ontology (systems) Overall conceptualization of a field of knowledge that may not be presented in a hierarchical manner (Jaspahara 2004, p. 93).

Operational definition The concrete and specific definition of something in terms of the *operations* by which observations are to be categorized (Babbie 1998).

An extensional definition hinged on measurable properties and leading to measurement operations. More broadly, a definition that establishes the meaning of the variable in terms of observable-measurable indicators (Sartori 1984, p. 80).

Operationalisation A theory that defines scientific concepts in terms of the actual experimental procedures used to establish their applicability (Dictionary of Modern Thought 1977, p. 612).

The creation of rules, which indicate when an instance of a concept has empirically occurred (Gill and Johnson 1991, p. 166).

One step beyond conceptualisation. It is the process of developing operational definitions (Babbie 1998).

To make a definition based on instructions for the operations that have to be done (Groot 1972, p. 232).

A doctrine mainly associated with a version of physics, that emphasizes the search for operational definitions of concepts (Bryman and Bell 2003, p. 69).

Ordinal measure A level of measurement describing a variable with attributes you can rank-order along some dimension. An example would be socio-economic status as composed of the attributes of high, medium, low. See also, nominal, interval, or ratio measures. Gender would be an example of nominal measure (Babbie 1998, p. G5).

An ordinal measure is a measure on ordinal scale. The ordinal scale includes the possibilities of the nominal scale (measurements in groups) and also allows ranking among the measurements, such as larger or smaller (Arbnor and Bjerke 1997, p. 230).

Paradigm Paradigm is nothing more than a perspective taken toward data, another analytic stance that helps to systematically gather and order data in such ways that structure and process are integrated (Strauss and Corbin 1998, p. 128).

Paradigm is a term, which is intended to emphasize the commonality of perspective, which binds the work of a group of theorists together in such a way that they can be usefully regarded as approaching social theory within the bounds of the same problematic (Burrel and Morgan 1979, p. 23).

Usually taken mean a way of looking at some phenomenon. A Perspective from which distinctive conceptualizations and explanations of phenomena are proposed (Gill and Johnson 1991, p. 166).

A paradigm may be viewed as a set of basic beliefs that deals with ultimate or first principles. It represent a worldview that defines, for its holder, the nature of the worldview that defines for its holder, the nature of the world, the individual place in it, and the range of possible relationships to that world and it parts (Denzin and Lincoln 1994, p. 107).

In Thomas Kuhn's sense, the scientific community consensus on what constitutes the scientific procedure, and the basic axioms or findings thus resulting. More loosely, a framework that gives organization and direction to scientific investigation (Sartori 1984, p. 80).

A term deriving from the history of science, where it was used to describe a cluster of beliefs and dictates that for scientists in a particular discipline influence what should be studied, how research should be done, and how results should be interpreted (Bryman and Bell 2003, p. 23).

Parsimony In quantitative social research refers to the use of as few independent variables as possible to explain as much of the variation in a dependent variable as possible (Ragin 1994, p. 189).

Parsimony (in definitions) A definition that includes only the necessary properties of a concept. Sartori (1984, p. 81).

Participative enquiry Participative enquiry is a phenomenological methodology and is about research with people rather than research on people. The participants in such a research study are involved as fully as possible in the research, which is conducted in their own group or organization. A member of the group may even initiate the research. Participants are involved in the data gathering and analysis. They also debate and determine the progress and direction of the research, thus enabling the researcher 'to evolve questions and answers as a shred experience with a group. There are three different approaches to participative enquiry: cooperative enquiry, participatory action research and action science. The basis for all these approaches is that they see 'human beings as co-creating their reality through participation, experience and action' (Hussey and Hussey 1997, p. 72).

Phenomenology Phenomenology is a presuppositionless philosophy which holds consciousness to be the matrix of all phenomena to be objects of intentional acts and treats them as essences, demands its own method, concerns itself with predicative experience, offers itself as the foundation of science, and comprises a philosophy of the life world, a defence of reason, and ultimately a critique of philosophy (Burrel and Morgan 1979, p. 232).

Phenomenology is the study of lived experiences and the ways we understand these experiences to develop a worldview (Marshall and Rossman 1999, p. 112).

Phenomenology seems to be the more prevailing approach to qualitative research in the social sciences literature (Gummesson 1991, p. 149).

A study of how things appear to people- how people experience the world (Gill and Johnson 1991, p. 166).

A qualitative research approach concerned with understanding certain group behaviours from that group's point of view. Copyright © 1997–2004 Colorado State University, http://writing.colostate.edu/guides/research/glossary/

Positivism The view that all true knowledge is scientific, in the sense of describing the co-existence and succession of observable phenomena (Dictionary of Modern Thought 1977, p. 668).

Knowledge consists of verified hypotheses that can be accepted as facts or laws (Denzin and Lincoln 1994, p. 113).

An approach that emphasizes the use of the methods presumed to be used in the natural sciences in the social sciences (Gill and Johnson 1991, p. 166).

This research tradition is based on the statistical analysis of data collected by means of descriptive and comparative studies and experiments (Gummeson 1991, p. 152).

A term with many uses in social science and philosophy. At the broad end it embraces any approach, which applies scientific method to human affairs conceived as belonging to a natural order open to objective enquiry. At the narrow end, Positivism is especially used in international relations to mean behaviourism so fierce it rejects all physiological data and qualitative data (Hollis 1994, p. 42).

An epistemological position that advocates the application of the methods of the natural sciences to the study of social reality and beyond (Bryman and Bell 2003, p. 14).

Precision One of the considerations in determining sample validity: the degree to which estimates from the sample reflect the measure taken by a census; measured by the standard error of the estimate – the smaller the error, the greater the precision of the estimate (Cooper and Schindler 2001, p. 165).

Prediction The use of accumulated social scientific knowledge about general patterns and past events to make projections or extrapolation about the future and other novel institutions. Generally, social researchers can make projections about rates and probabilities, but not about specific events, like the timing of a major political change (Ragin 1994, pp. 189–190).

Problem classification To classify a problem in terms of the nature of the decision makers and in terms of the nature of the system(s) in which the problem is located (Flood and Jackson 1991, p. 141).

Problem (definition) The issue that exists in the literature, theory, or practice that leads to a need for the study (Creswell 1994, p. 50).

A problem is a situation or a state of affairs that causes difficulties for people, so that they try to think of a way to deal with it (Collins Cobuild Dictionary 1987, p. 1143).

A problem is defined as the difference between what is (or will be) and what we would like the situation to be (Easton 1992, p. 13).

The interpretation, (empirical) grounding and 'labelling' of a situation, condition, phenomenon or function of the organization that is experienced as problematic by those involved to such an extent that it requires research with regard to (possible) solutions.

The total reasoning by means of which the researcher defines the phenomenon to be examined into a (scientific) researchable (and relevant) research problem.

Problem fields Are the metaphorical pastures in which problems roam (Thomas 2004, p. 26).

Problems (functional and instrumental) Instrumental and functional problems have a causal relation. An instrumental problem concerns causes. Functional problems concern the undesired effects in terms of the desired performance (Leeuw 2000, p. 288).

Problems (goal) Problems that occur because the problem owner desires unfeasible and unrealistic goals (Leeuw 2000, p. 283).

Problem owners People who are assigned 'rights of ownership' of a problem, voluntarily or obligatory. He who has feeling of unease about a situation, either a sense of mismatch between 'what is' and 'what might be' or a vague feeling that things could be better and who wishes something were done about it (Checkland 1999, p. 294).

Problem identification During this stage a problem must be identified as a candidate for research and evaluated to assess its suitability before resources are allocated to pursuing it (Thomas 2004, p. 26).

In research settings, this might involve defining the problem form a number of perspectives, using different theoretical frameworks to investigate a problem, and having different and opposing viewpoints to solving problem (Cunningham 1993, p. 57).

Problems (perception) Problems that (to the judgment of the investigator) can (must) be solved by changing the perception (Leeuw 2000, p. 282).

Perceptions act as a filter to information from the 'action world' and determine what information is significant. Each person perceives 'reality' in different ways (Jayaratna 1994, p. 65).

Problems (reality) It is a problem, which arises in the everyday world of events and ideas, and may be perceived differently by different people. Such problems are not constructed by the investigators (Checkland 1999, p. 316).

Problem for what the solution has to be found in changing the reality. Reality problems are control problems for the problem owner (Leeuw 2000, p. 284).

Problem (statements) The problem statement needs to convince the sponsor to continue reading. It contains the need for the research project. The problem is usually represented by a management question and is followed by a more detailed set of objectives (Cooper and Schindler 2003, p. 101, 662).

Quasi-experiment In an experiment, subjects are pre-tested and then randomly assigned to a treatment group or a control group. In a post-test, the two groups are compared to ascertain the impact of the treatment. True experiments must be constructed but comparative politics can occasionally take advantage of naturally occurring quasi-experiments to draw inferences about the impact of a particular variable (for example, electoral reform) (Hague et al. 1998, p. 279).

Questionnaire A document containing questions and other types of items designed to solicit information appropriate to analysis. *Questionnaires* are used primarily in survey research and also in experiments, field research, and other modes of observation. Comparative Methods Dictionary, http://poli.haifa.ac.il/~levi/dictionary.html

Question (closed) A question that contains a clear outline and is therefore suitable for further delineation.
 A type of measurement question that presents the respondent with a fixed set of questions (nominal, ordinal, or interval data) (Cooper and Schindler 2001, p. 334).
 A question employed in an interview schedule or self-completion questionnaire that presents the respondent with a set of possible answers to choose from. Also called fixed-choice question and pre-coded question (Bryman and Bell 2003, p. 116).

Question (open) Open questions give the respondent the possibility to answer with a personal response or opinion in his or her own words. Open questions offer the advantage that the respondents are able to give their opinions as precisely as possible in their own words, but they can be difficult to analyze. In a questionnaire survey, open questions may deter busy respondents from replying to the questionnaire (Hussey and Hussey 1997, p. 166).

Random sample A sample in which every member of the population (simple random sample) or some subset of the population (stratified sample) being tested has an equal chance of being included in the sample. The purpose of sampling is to be able to infer, from the sample taken, the attributes of the population as a whole. Only if the sample is random can the probability be calculated that a sampled attribute applies to the population as a whole. Comparative Methods Dictionary, http://poli.haifa.ac.il/~levi/dictionary.html
 A question that concerns a broad definition of a problem that offers all opportunity for interpretation and outline.
 A type of measurement question in which the respondent provides the answer without the aid of an interviewer (either in phone, personal interview, or self-administered surveys); a.k.a. unstructured or free response question (nominal, ordinal or ratio data) (Cooper and Schindler 2001, p. 345).
 A question employed in an interview schedule or self-completion questionnaire that does not present the respondent with a set of possible answers to choose from (Bryman and Bell 2003, p. 117).

Ratio measure A level of measurement describing a variable the attributes of which have all the qualities of ordinal, interval, or nominal measures and in addition are based on a 'true zero' point. Age would be an example of a ratio measure (Babbie 1998, p. G6).

Realism May be divided into metaphysical realism and epistemological realism. The former consider that reality exists independently of the cognitive structures of observers, while the latter considers that reality is cognitively accessible to observers. Much of realism entails both views, although some realists would claim that, while reality does exist and dependently of our efforts to understand it, it is not cognitively accessible (Gill and Johnson 1991, p. 166).
 An epistemological position that acknowledges a reality independent of the senses that is accessible to the researchers tools and theoretical speculations. It implies that the categories created by the scientists refer to real objects in the natural or social worlds (Bryman and Bell 2003, p. 15).

Reflection A reflection is something, which informs you about a particular thing because it has similar characteristics or because it is based on that other thing (Collins Cobuild Dictionary 1987, p. 1210).

Reflexivity A term used in research methodology to refer to a reflectiveness among social researchers about the implications for the knowledge of the social world they generate of their methods, values, biases, decisions, and mere presence in the very situations they investigate (Bryman and Bell 2003, p. 529).

It is the monitoring by an ethnographer of his or her impact upon the social situation under investigation. So rather than to attempt to eliminate the effects of the researcher on the investigation, the researcher should attempt to understand his or her effect upon, and role in, n the research setting and utilize this knowledge to elicit data (Gill and Johnson 2002, p. 147, 228).

Reflexivity is the process through which a researcher recognizes, examines, and understands how his or her own social background and assumptions can intervene in the research process. It is sensitivity to the important situational dynamics between the researcher and researched that can impact the creation of knowledge. Researchers can use the process of reflexivity as a tool to assist them with studying across difference (Heasse-Biber and Leavy 2006, p. 146).

Reduction Questioning or interrogating the meanings or categories that have been developed. Are there any other ways of looking at the data?

Process of selecting, abstracting, from raw data to written data.

Reduction (selective) The central idea of content analysis. Text is reduced to categories consisting of a word, set of words or phrases, on which the researcher can focus. Specific words or patterns are indicative of the research question and determine levels of analysis and generalization. Copyright © 1997–2004 Colorado State University, http://writing.colostate.edu/guides/research/glossary/

Reductionism Strict limitation (reduction) of the kinds of concepts to be considered relevant to the phenomenon under study (Babbie 1998).

Reification The process of regarding things that are not real as real (Babbie 1998).

The apprehension of human phenomena as if they were things, that is, in non-human or possibly supra-human terms (Berger and Luckman 1966).

The apprehension of the products of human activity as if they were something else than human products – such as facts of nature, results of cosmic laws, or manifestations of divine will (Berger and Luckmann 1966).

Relativism The notion that how things appear to people, and individual's judgment about truth, is relative to their particular paradigm or frame of reference (Gill and Johnson 1991, p. 166).

Reliability Will the measure yield the same results on different occasions (assuming no real change in what is to be measured).

Will different researchers make similar observations on different occasions?

The statements have to be based on an accurate observation of reality and should not have their origins in accidental circumstances in the instruments of measurement, nor in the examined unities.

The extent to which findings can be replicated, or reproduced, by another inquirer (Denzin and Lincoln 1994, p. 100).

A criterion that refers to the consistency of the results obtained in research (Gill and Johnson 1991, p. 166).

The extent to which a measure, procedure or instrument yields the same result on repeated trials. Copyright © 1997–2004 Colorado State University, http://writing.colostate.edu/guides/research/glossary/

That quality of measurement method that suggests that the same data would have been collected each time in repeated observations of the same phenomenon (Babbie 1998).

The extent to which measurements yield, when repeated, similar or confirming results (Sartori 1984, p. 82).

Consistency in performance or prediction (Salkind 2000, p. 106).

The degree to which a measure of a concept is stable (Bryman and Bell 2003, p. 76).

A characteristic of measurement concerned with accuracy, precision, and consistency; a necessary but not sufficient condition for validity (if the measure is not reliable, it cannot be valid) (Cooper and Schindler 2001, p. 215).

Reliability (Cronbach's alpha) A commonly used test of internal reliability. It essentially calculates the average of all possible split-half reliability coefficients. A computed alpha coefficient will vary between 1 (denoting perfect internal reliability) and 0 (denoting no internal reliability). The figure 0.80 is typically employed as a rule of thumb to denote an acceptable level of internal reliability (Bryman and Bell 2003, p. 77).

Reliability (stability) The agreement of measuring instruments over time. Copyright © 1997–2004 Colorado State University, http://writing.colostate.edu/guides/research/glossary/

Replication Generally, the duplication of an experiment to expose or reduce error. It is also a technical term used in connection with the elaboration model, referring to the elaboration outcome in which the initially observed relationship between two variables persists when a *control variable* is held constant (Babbie 1998).

Research design A research design describes a flexible set of guidelines that connect theoretical paradigms to strategies of inquiry and methods for collecting empirical material (Denzin and Lincoln 1994, p. 14).

A plan for collecting and analyzing evidence that will make it possible for the investigator to answer whatever questions he or she has posed. The design of an investigation touches almost all aspects of the research, form the minute details of data collection to the selection of the techniques of data analysis (Ragin 1994, p. 191).

A framework for the collection and analysis of data. A choice of research design reflects decisions about the priority being given to a range of dimensions of the research process (such as causality and generalization) (Bryman and Bell 2003, p. 32).

The blueprint for fulfilling research objectives and answering questions (Cooper and Schindler 2001, p. 75).

Research (empirical) The process of developing systematized knowledge gained from observations that are formulated to support insights and generalizations about the phenomena under study. (Lauer and Asher 1988, p. 7). Copyright © 1997–2004 Colorado State University, http://writing.colostate.edu/guides/research/glossary/

Research (qualitative) Empirical research in which the researcher explores relationships using textual, rather than quantitative data. Case study, observation, and ethnography are considered forms of qualitative research. Results are not usually considered generalizable, but are often transferable. Copyright © 1997–2004 Colorado State University, http://writing.colostate.edu/guides/research/glossary/

A basic strategy of social research that usually involves in-depth examination of a relatively small number of cases. Cases are examined intensively with techniques designed to facilitate the clarification of theoretical concepts and empirical categories (Ragin 1994, p. 190).

Research (quantitative) Empirical research in which the researcher explores relationships using numeric data. Survey is generally considered a form of quantitative research. Results can often be generalized, though this is not always the case. Copyright © 1997–2004 Colorado State University, http://writing.colostate.edu/guides/research/glossary/

A basic strategy of social research that usually involves analysis of patterns of co variation across a large number of cases. This approach focuses on variables and relationships among variables in an effort to identify general patterns of co-variation (Ragin 1994, p. 190).

Research strategies Combine a primary research objective and a specific research method, for example, the use of comparative methods to study diversity. Each strategy constitutes a specific way of linking ideas and evidence to produce a representation of some aspect of social life (Ragin 1994, p. 191).

Retroduction The interplay of induction and deduction, and is central to the process of scientific discovery. The process of constructing representations form the interaction between analytic frames and images involves retroduction (Ragin 1994, p. 191).

Rhetoric A concern with the ways in which appeals to convince or persuade are devised (Bryman and Bell 2003, p. 519).

Rich picture A cartoon-like expression, in the spirit of such representations, allows for certain issues, conflicts and other problematic and interesting features to be accentuated. The rich picture expression represents the climate of the situation (Flood and Jackson 1991, p. 172).

It is a graphical summary of the main factors affecting a situation (Patching 1990, p. 280).

Rigor Degree to which research methods are scrupulously and meticulously carried out in order to recognize important influences occurring in an experiment. Copyright © 1997–2004 Colorado State University, http://writing.colostate.edu/guides/research/glossary/

Sample The population researched in a particular study. Usually, attempts are made to select a 'sample population' that is considered representative of groups of people to whom results will be generalized or transferred. In studies that use inferential statistics to analyze results or which are designed to be generalisable, sample size is critical – generally the larger the number in the sample, the higher the likelihood of a representative distribution of the population. Copyright © 1997–2004 Colorado State University, http://writing.colostate.edu/guides/research/glossary/

Saturation Saturation is the process or state that occurs when one thing is filled so full of another thing that no more can be added (Collins Cobuild Dictionary 1987, p. 1286).

When additional analysis no longer contributes to discovering anything new about a category (Strauss 1987, p. 21).

The diminishing marginal contribution of each additional case (Gummeson 1991, p. 85).

Sensitising concepts A term devised by Blumer to refer to a preference for treating a concept as a guide in an investigation, so that it points in a general way to what is relevant or important. This position contrasts with the idea of an operational definition, in which the meaning of a concept is fixed in advance of carrying out an investigation (Bryman and Bell 2003, p. 286).

It gives the user a general sense of reference and guidance in approaching empirical instances. Whereas definitive concepts provided prescriptions of what to see, sensitizing concepts merely suggest directions along which to look (Blumer 1954).

Sensitizing Concepts are theory-embedded notions used by the researcher (f/m) when studying phenomenon in the case(s).

Sensitizing Concepts are pre-theoretical by nature and guide the way of looking.

Sensitivity (context) Awareness by a qualitative researcher of factors such as values and beliefs that influence cultural behaviours. Copyright © 1997–2004 Colorado State University, http://writing.colostate.edu/guides/research/glossary/

Survey A research tool that includes at least one question that is either open-ended or close-ended and employs an oral or written method for asking these questions. The goal of a survey is to gain specific information about either a specific group or a representative sample of a particular group. Results are typically used to understand the attitudes, beliefs, or knowledge of a particular group. Copyright © 1997–2004 Colorado State University, http://writing.colostate.edu/guides/research/glossary/

Techniques A technique is a particular method of doing an activity, usually a method that involves practical skills (Collins Cobuild Dictionary 1987, p. 1501).

Teleology The theory that events can only be explained, and that evaluation of anything can only be justified, by consideration of the ends towards, which they are directed (Dictionary of Modern Thought 1977, p. 861).

Teleology is the theory or belief that all natural things are designed to fulfil a particular purpose (Collins Cobuild Dictionary 1987, p. 1502).

Greek telos, 'end'; logos, 'discourse', in philosophy, the science or doctrine that attempts to explain the universe in terms of ends or final causes. Teleology is based on the proposition that the universe has design and purpose. In Aristotelian philosophy, the explanation of, or justification for, a phenomenon or process is to be found not only in the immediate purpose or cause, but also in the 'final cause' – the reason for which the phenomenon exists or was created. In Christian theology, teleology represents a basic argument for the existence of God, in that the order and efficiency of the natural world seem not to be accidental. If the world design is intelligent, an ultimate Designer must exist.

Teleologists oppose mechanistic interpretations of the universe that rely solely on organic development or natural causation. The powerful impact of Charles Darwin's theories of evolution, which hold that species develop by natural selection, has greatly reduced the influence of traditional teleological arguments. Nonetheless, such arguments were still advanced by many during the upsurge of creationist sentiment in the early 1980s (Brown and Novick 1997).

Testability A procedure for critical evaluation; a means of determining the presence, quality, or truth of something; a trial. The American Heritage: Dictionary (2000).

Theoretical sampling A deliberate selection of cases. Theoretical sampling describes the process of choosing new research sites of cases to compare with one that has already been studied. For example, a researcher interested in how environmental activists in the United States maintain their political commitments might extend the study to (1) environmental activists in another part of the world or perhaps to (2) another type of activist. The goal of theoretical sampling is not to sample in a way that captures all possible variations, rather in one that aids the development of concepts and deepens the understanding of research subjects (Ragin 1994, p. 98).

Theory A Theory is an idea or set of ideas that is intended to explain something. It is based on evidence and careful reasoning but it cannot be completely proved (Collins Cobuild Dictionary 1987, p. 1515).

A formulation regarding the cause and effect relationship between two or more variables, which may or may not have been tested (Gill and Johnson 1991, p. 166).

A system of ideas, which conceptualises some aspect of experience (Dey 1993, p. 276).

Compare with Sartori – a body of systematically related generalizations of explanatory value (Sartori 1984, p. 84).

A group of logically related statements that explain things that have occurred in the past and predicts things that will occur in the future (Salkind 2000, p. 3).

A set of systematically integrated concepts, definitions, and propositions that are advanced to explain or predict phenomena (facts); the generalizations we make about variables and the relationships among variables (Cooper 2001, p. 51).

Theory: *middle range theory* Theorizing can be performed at several levels of social inquiry. The midpoint between micro-level and macro-level theories is where middle-range theories are located. Robert Merton suggested that middle-range theories represent the most constructive effort for theorizing. It is in the middle between the minor working hypotheses and the all-inclusive speculations were one can hope to derive a very large number of empirically observed uniformities of social behaviour. Comparative Methods Dictionary, http://poli.haifa.ac.il/~levi/dictionary.html

Theory-laden This term refers to the way in which the prior values, knowledge and theories of an observer influence what he or she sees during observation (Gill and Johnson 1991, p. 166).

The property of observations varying with or depending upon the theoretical commitments of the observer. Insofar as observations are theory laden, your beliefs – as shaped by the theory or paradigm you accept – determine what you observe, so that partisans of different theories (or paradigms) will observe differently (Leiber 2001).

Theory-testing It involves deducing how the world should look if the theory's prepositions are valid and then setting out to obtain data to see if reality matches expectations (Thomas 2004, p. 17).

Transferability To allow readers to explore the extent to which the study may, or may not, have applicability beyond the specific context within which the data were generated; the researcher should report the contextual features of the study in full.

The ability to apply the results of research in one context to another similar context. Also, the extent to which a study invites readers to make connections between elements of the study and their own experiences. Copyright © 1997–2004 Colorado State University, http://writing.colostate.edu/guides/research/glossary/

Triangulation Triangulation is used for the application of two or more methods on the same research problem in order to increase the reliability of the results (Gummeson 1991, p. 122).

The use of different research methods in the same study to collect data so as to check validity of any findings. The collection of different data upon the same phenomena, something using different researchers so as to validity any findings. Collecting data upon the same phenomenon at different times and places within the same study (Gill and Johnson 1991, p. 166).

The use of a combination of research methods in a study. An example of triangulation would be a study that incorporated surveys, interviews, and observations. Copyright © 1997–2004 Colorado State University, http://writing.colostate.edu/guides/research/glossary/

The use of more than one method or source of data in the study of a social phenomenon so that findings may be cross-checked (Bryman and Bell 2003, p. 291).

Triangulation in quantitative research Using, involving and combining different (data) sources in order to show that similar results have been produced.

Triangulation in qualitative research Using, involving and combining different (data) sources in order to reflect upon several facts simultaneously. There are four basic forms of triangulation: data-triangulation, researchers-triangulation and methodological triangulation.

Typology The classification of observations in terms of their attributes on two or more variables. The classification of newspapers as liberal-urban, liberal-rural, conservative-urban or conservative-rural would be an example (Babbie 1998).

Units of analysis The *what* or *whom* being studied. In social science research, the most typical units of analysis are individual people (Babbie 1998).

Units of analysis are related to the fundamental problem of defining what the 'case' is. The case can be an individual or an event or entity that is less well defined than an individual. The selection of the appropriate units of analysis will occur when the primary research question is accurately specified (Yin 2003, p. 23, 24).

Usability The quality of a design is its usability. A design is usable (relevant and valid) if it does that what it has been made for, under the circumstances it has it has been designed for and against reasonable costs (Leeuw 2000, p. 214).

Utility Is for the researcher after all a central requirement, but it needs to be recognized as not a single idea – useful for whom, and for what purpose? Additionally, utility has its own limitations: other requirements of management research are not automatically determined by the practicality test (Griseri 2002, p. 56).

Validation The process by which scientific theories become accepted. Comparative Methods Dictionary, http://poli.haifa.ac.il/~levi/dictionary.html

Validation (communicative) A dialogue among those considered legitimate knower who may often make competing claims to knowledge building. The idea is that each interpretation of a given finding is open to discussion and refutation by the wider community of researchers, and sometimes this extends to community in which the research itself was conducted (Hesse-Biber and Leavy 2006, p. 64).

Validation (explanatory) The commonest definition of validity is epitomized by the question: Are we measuring what we think we are measuring? (Kerlinger 1973, p. 457).

Validity (concurrent) Concurrent validity measures the description of the present (Cooper 2003, p. 232).

Validation (external) The process of testing the validity of a measure, such as an index or scale, by examining its relationship to other, presumed indicators of the same variable. If the index really measures prejudice, for example, it should correlate with other indicators of prejudice (Babbie 1998).

Does an observed causal relationship generalize across persons, settings and times (Cooper 2003, p. 432).

Validity (discriminate) Comparison is between measures of unrelated ideas test the measure's validity, which is its ability to distinguish the phenomenon it claims to measure from other phenomena to which it is supposedly irrelevant (Brewer and Hunter 2006, p. 111).

Validity (predictive) Predictive validity measures the prediction of the future (Cooper 2003, p. 232).

How well does it predict performance on the criterion in question; this is called predictive criterion validity (Robson 2002, p. 103).

Validity (general) The characteristics of an inference whose conclusion must be true if its premises are (Dictionary of Modern Thought 1977, p. 906).

The degree to which a study accurately reflects or assesses the specific concept that the researcher is attempting to measure. A method can be reliable, consistently measuring the same thing, but not valid. See also internal validity and external validity. Copyright © 1997–2004 Colorado State University, http://writing.colostate.edu/guides/research/glossary/

Describes assertions, arguments, conclusions, reasons, or intellectual processes that are persuasive because they are well founded. What is valid is based on or borne out by truth or fact or has legal force (The American Heritage: Dictionary 2000).

Refers to the appropriateness of a measure – does it measure what it is supposed to measure? To assess validity researchers must assess whether their data collection and measurement procedures work the way they claim (Ragin 1994, p. 193).

A characteristic of measurement concerned that a test measures what the researcher actually wishes to measure; that difference found with a measurement tool reflect true differences with among respondents drawn from a population (Cooper and Schindler 2001, p. 211).

A concern with the integrity of the conclusions that are generated from a piece of research. When used on its own, validity is usually taken to refer to measurement validity (Bryman and Bell 2003, p. 77).

The truthfulness or accuracy within the score of a test or interpretation of an experiment (Salkind 2000, p. 113).

Validity (convergent) The general agreement among ratings, gathered independently of one another, where measures should be theoretically related. Copyright © 1997–2004 Colorado State University, http://writing.colostate.edu/guides/research/glossary/

Validity (discriminate) The lack of a relationship among measures which theoretically should not be related. Copyright © 1997–2004 Colorado State University, http://writing.colostate.edu/guides/research/glossary/

Validity (construct) Do items measure hypothetical constructs or concepts? (Creswell 1994, p. 121).

Seeks an agreement between a theoretical concept and a specific measuring device, such as observation. Copyright © 1997–2004 Colorado State University, http://writing.colostate.edu/guides/research/glossary/

It is a quantitative question rather than a qualitative distinction. It can be measured by the correlation between the intended independent variable (construct) and the proxy independent variable (indicator, sign) that is actually used (Hunter and Schmidt 1990).

Construct validation is involved whenever a test is to be interpreted as a measure of some attribute or quality, which is not 'operationally defined.' The problem faced by the investigator is, 'What constructs account for variance in test performance?' (Cronbach and Meehl 1955, pp. 281–302).

Validity (Internal) The degree to which findings correctly map the phenomenon in question (Denzin and Lincoln 1994, p. 100).

An assessment of the degree of isomorphism between a study's findings and the real world (Guba and Lincoln 1989, p. 236).

The extents to which the conclusions regarding cause and effect are warranted (Denzin and Lincoln 1994, p. 100).

(1) The rigor with which the study was conducted (e.g. the study's design, the care taken to conduct measurements, and decisions concerning what was and wasn't measured) and (2) the extent to which the designers of a study have taken into account alternative explanations for any causal relationships they explore (Huitt 1998).

In studies that do not explore causal relationships, only the first of these definitions should be considered when assessing internal validity. Copyright © 1997–2004 Colorado State University, http://writing.colostate.edu/guides/research/glossary/

The process whereby the individual items composing a composite measure are correlated with the measure itself. This provides one test of the wisdom of including all the items in the composite measure (Babbie 1998).

Validity (external) The degree to which findings can be generalized to other settings similar to the one in which the study occurred (Denzin and Lincoln 1994, p. 100).

A concepts that embodies the very essence of generaliziability, likewise can have little meaning if the realities to which one might wish to generalize exist in different value systems (Guba and Lincoln 1989, p. 236).

The extent to which the results of a study are generalizable or transferable. See also validity. Copyright © 1997–2004 Colorado State University, http://writing.colostate.edu/guides/research/glossary/

Validity (content) Do the items measure the content they were intended to measure? (Creswell 1994, p. 121).

The extent to which a measurement reflects the specific intended domain of content (Carmines and Zeller 1991, p. 20). Copyright © 1997–2004 Colorado State University, http://writing.colostate.edu/guides/research/glossary/

Content validity is concerned with sample-population representativeness, i.e. the knowledge and skills covered by the test items should be representative to the larger domain of knowledge and skills (Cronbach 1971).

Validity (predictive) Do scores predict a criterion measure? Creswell (1994, p. 121).

Validity (concurrent) Do result correlate with each other? Creswell (1994, p. 121).

Validity (face) Do the items appear to measure what the instrument purports to measure? Creswell (1994, p. 121).

Face validity simply means the validity at face value. As a check on face validity, test/survey items are sent to teachers to obtain suggestions for modification. Because of its vagueness and subjectivity, psychometricians have abandoned this concept for a long time (Cronbach 1971).

Face validity is concerned with how a measure or procedure appears. Does it seem like a reasonable way to gain the information the researchers are attempting to obtain? Does it seem well designed? Does it seem as though it will work reliably? Unlike content validity, face validity does not depend on established theories for support (Fink 1995).

That quality of an indicator that makes it seems a reasonable measure of some variable. That the frequency of church attendance is some indication of a person's religiosity seems to make sense without a lot of explanation. It has *face validity* (Babbie 1998, p. G3).

Validity (population) The extent to which conclusions might be generalized to other people (Gill and Johnson 1991, p. 166).

The extent to which the results of a study can be generalized from the specific sample that was studied to a larger group of subjects (Bracht and Glass 1968, pp. 437–474).

Validity (ecological) The extent to which conclusions might be generalized to social contexts other than those in which data has been collected (Gill and Johnson 1991, p. 166).

The extent to which the results of an experiment can be generalized from the set of environmental conditions created by the researcher to other environmental conditions (settings and conditions) (Bracht and Glass 1968, pp. 437–474).

Validity (criterion related) Used to demonstrate the accuracy of a measuring procedure by comparing it with another procedure, which has been demonstrated to be valid; also referred to as instrumental validity. Copyright © 1997–2004 Colorado State University, http://writing. colostate.edu/guides/research/glossary/

Variable (general) A concept, which varies by kind or amount (Dey 1993, p. 276).

Variance A measure of the degree of dispersion of a series of numbers around their mean. The larger the variance the greater the spread of the series around its means. Comparative Methods Dictionary, http://poli.haifa.ac.il/~levi/dictionary.html

The variance is the average of the squared deviation scores form the distribution's mean. It is a measure of score dispersion from the mean. The greater the dispersion of scores, the greater is the variance (Cooper and Schindler 2003, p. 475).

Verification Testing the empirical validity of assertions, generalizations, laws and theories. Since the number of supporting instances is indefinite, a process of verification is never final (Satori 1984, p. 85).

Variable (exogenous) A variable whose value is not determined with the set of equations, or models, established to make predictions or test a hypothesis. Comparative Methods Dictionary, http://poli.haifa.ac.il/~levi/dictionary.html

Variable (nominal) A variable determined by categories, which cannot be ordered, e.g. gender and colour. Copyright © 1997–2004 Colorado State University, http://writing.colostate.edu/ guides/research/glossary/

Verstehen The value of subjective evidence to the value of evidence from the accused and the victim in a court of law.

A method of analysis particularly suited to the investigation of social affairs, for which the subjective meanings of events are all important (Burrel and Morgan 1979, p. 83).

Term used in Germany from the late nineteenth century to denote understanding within, by means of empathy, intuition or imagination, as opposed to knowledge from without, by means of observation or calculation (Dictionary of Modern Thought 1977, p. 908).

A term used to explain the actions of subjects by understanding the subjective dimensions of their behaviour (Gill and Johnson 1991, p. 166).

The value of subjective evidence is analogous to the value of evidence from the accused and the victim in a court of law (Vygotski 1993, p. 276).

Chapter 10
Epilogue

Research is above all a social activity in containing an array of ideas, concepts and instruments that can be applied in many different ways. The previous chapters have demonstrated the difficulty of constructing a sound research design given the array of possible choices. We have called this equifinality. Being novices to the research field we perfectly understand that many students find it difficult to make well-reasoned choices – to act upon their own basic and often only recently acquired (research) attitude and make methodological choices of which they cannot accurately appraise the implications. It should come as no surprise that stimulated by the preferences of a supervisor time and again the same methodological set is applied often driven by a justification based on replicability, robustness or reliability. The premise that a research project marks the end of a programme that has taught the student to develop and demonstrate his ability to do sound research is false. We believe that for many students it is only *after* the research project itself that students really come to understand what it is to engage in research, because they have discovered and experienced firsthand the methodological, theoretical and practical connotations.

The idea that scientific research is a neutral, objective search for the 'truth' is hardly credible in the social sciences at large. Any scholarly publication elaborating on the philosophy of knowledge – the different epistemological debates and competing paradigms –will demonstrate this perspective. Recognising and understanding the difficulties that come with this view and knowing how to address them becomes an important component of the research itself. It is crucial to learn how to select and justify the appropriate mix of methodology, methods and techniques that support a specific approach for conducting research in a specific context. In the preceding chapter we have pieced this approach together from a variety of sources and our own experiences – as teachers and researchers. The results are certainly not free from internal contradiction and as such open to debate. It represents what we think many students actually ought to do as opposed to what they claim they do and in that sense forms a benchmark for judging actual practice in applied research (Ryan 1992).

J. Jonker and B. Pennink, *The Essence of Research Methodology*,
DOI 10.1007/978-3-540-71659-4_10, © Springer-Verlag Berlin Heidelberg 2010

Students in management sciences mainly conduct research in organisations addressing problems derived from others' ambition to organise their organisations better. Their research generally focuses on why given a particular situation a problem surfaces and seems to be in need of a solution. Why the organising actually takes place or what the underlying concepts, ideas and assumptions are, is not the actual object of the research. The aim is to understand why problems emerge so that knowledge of the theory and practice of organising is essential. Organising nowadays has moved from a functional and rationalist approach towards one in which an infinite universe of possible organisational constructs are possible. This development – rather transitional in nature – demands the development of a corresponding body of theory. Needless to say theory development for this new branch of management sciences provides challenging opportunities. In the everyday practice of applied research, scrutinising theory, however, does not seem to be the core issue. A conceptual model – as a ready-made abstraction of 'reality' – seems to be a more meaningful and handy concept for students when they are learning to handle the notion of theory. As we have argued the theoretical scope of any model is defined by its assumptions and attendant set of explanatory or predictive implications. Understanding the theoretical nature of an applied model is essential. Elaborating and scrutinising on that embedded theoretical body of knowledge may be even more important.

This text as a whole is rather constructivist in tone although not naively so. This is our philosophical perspective of organising. Organising represents the continuous construction of interactions with the various and sometimes-conflicting goals of the stakeholders in mind. Although an array of established conceptual models can be distinguished to address specific organisational issues the actual act of organising remains fundamentally social. Time after time, people create what we have come to call 'the organisation' – a reification that certainly serves its purpose but is not accurate when it comes to understanding what organising is all about. Organising has been defined as an ongoing stream of events in which people make deliberate and intuitive choices to alter the chain of events. But what we organise when we organise often remains 'a riddle wrapped in an enigma'. Truly understanding why a specific problem – or maybe it is better to speak of a configuration of problems – needs to be addressed at a specific moment remains a core issue throughout any research. The biggest pitfall here is to 'fix' the problem at the beginning of the research and not to handle it throughout the process of the research as a capricious 'creature'.

The key to selecting and applying a specific methodology to deal with a particular question lies in understanding the nature of the assumptions that come with it. Good research is determined by how the connection between data, analysis and theory is being demonstrated and justified. We have strongly argued that meaning is given to data in terms of the theories concerned. For any set of data a number of inevitably ambiguous relations can be created to support different theoretical concepts. This reflects the fact that data can take on radically different interpretations when viewed from different theoretical perspectives although the people involved may well agree on the reliability of the data itself. That is the freedom of the researcher, yet it is a freedom that demands lucidity, clear arguments and professionalism in its application. Learning to justify one's research actions and choices in a transparent manner seems to be the cornerstone of sound applied research. We do hope this text has contributed to this understanding.

References Glossary

Arbnor, I. & Bjerke, B. (1997). *Methodology for creating business knowledge*. London: Sage.

Babbie, E. (1998). *The practice of social research*. Wadsworth: G3 Publishing Company.

Barton Cunningham, J. (1993). *Action research and organizational development*. Westport: Greenwood Publishing.

Baumard, P. (1999). *Tacit knowledge in organizations*. London: Sage.

Berger, P. L. & Luckmann, T. (1966). *The social construction of reality*. New York: Anchor Books.

Blackburn, S. (1996). *The Oxford dictionary of philosophy*. Oxford: Oxford University Press.

Bracht, G. H. & Glass, G. V. (1968). The external validity of experiments. *American Education Research Journal, 5*, 437–474.

Brewer, J. & Hunter, A. (1989). *Multi-method research*. Thousand Oaks, CA: Sage.

Brewer, J. & Hunter, A. (2006). *Foundations of multi-method research, synthesizing styles*. London: Sage.

Brown, D. J. & McClen Novick, R. (eds). (1997). *Mavericks of the mind: Conversations for the New Millennium*. Freedom: Crossing Press.

Bryman, A. (2004). *Social research methods*. Oxford: Oxford University Press.

Bryman, A. & Bell, E. (2003). *Business research methods*. New York: Oxford University Press.

Bullock, A. & Trombley, S. (eds). (1977). *The new dictionary of modern thought*. London: HarperCollins Publishers.

Burrel, G. & Morgan, G. (1979). *Sociological paradigms and organizational analysis*. Hants: Gower Publishing.

Cassell, C. & Symon, G. (1994). *Qualitative methods in organizational research*. London: Sage.

Checkland, P. (1999). *Systems thinking, systems practice*. West Sussex: Wiley.

Choo, C. W. (1998). *The knowing organization*. New York: Oxford University Press.

Cobuild, C. (1987). *English language dictionary*. London: Harper Collins Publishers.

Conbach, L. J. & Meehl, P. E. (1955). Construct validity in psychological tests. *Psychological Bulletin, 52*, 281–302.

Cooper, D. R. & Schindler, P. S. (2001). *Business research methods*. New York: McGraw-Hill.

Creswell, J. W. (1994). *Research design: qualitative & quantitative approaches*. London: Sage.

Cronbach, L. J. (1971). Test validation. In R. L. Thorndike (Ed.), *Educational measurement* (2nd ed.). Washington, DC: American Council on Education.

Cunningham, J. B. (1993). *Action research and organizational development*. Westport: Praeger Publishers.

de Groot, A. D. (1972). *Methodologie*. Den Haag: Mouton and Company.

de Leeuw, A. C. J. (2000). *Bedrijfskundig management*. Assen: Koninklijke van Gorcum and Company.

Denzin, N. K. & Lincoln, Y. S. (1994). *Handbook of qualitative research*. Thousand Oaks, CA: Sage.

Dey, I. (1993). *Qualitative data analysis. A User-Friendly guide for social scientists*. London: Routledge.

Dogan, M. & Pelassy, D. (1984). *How to compare nations: strategies in comparative politics*. New Jersey: Chatham House Publishers.

Easton, G. (1992). *Learning from case studies*. London: Prentice Hall.

Elster, J. (1989). *Nuts and bolts for the social sciences*. Cambridge: Cambridge University Press.

Fink, A. (ed). (1995). *How to measure survey reliability and validity*. Thousand Oaks, CA: Sage.

Flood, R. L. & Jackson, M. C. (1991). *Creative problem solving*. West Sussex: Wiley.

Franssen, M. (1997). *Some contributions to methodological individualism in the social sciences*. PhD Dissertation, University of Amsterdam.

Gill, J. & Johnson, P. (1991). *Research methods for managers*. London: Paul Chapman Publishing.

Gill, J. & Johnson, P. (2002). *Research methods for managers*. London: Sage.

Goertz, G. (2006). *Social science concepts. A user's guide*. New Jersey: Princeton University Press.

Greenwood, D. J. & Levin, M. (1998). *Introduction to action research; social research for social change*. London: Sage.

Griseri, P. (2002). *Management knowledge, a critical view*. New York: Palgrave.

Guba, E. G. & Lincoln, Y. S. (1989). *Fourth generation evaluation*. London: Sage.

Gummesson, E. (1991). *Qualitative methods in management research*. London: Sage.

Hague, R., Harrop, M., & Breslin, S. (1998). *Comparative government and politics: an introduction* (4th ed.). Basingstoke: Palgrave.

Hedström, P. (2003). Generative models and explanatory research: On the sociology of Aage B. Sørensen. In A. L. Kalleberg et al (Eds.), *Inequality: structures, dynamics and mechanisms: essays in honor of Aage B Sørensen*. Special issue of *Research in Social Stratification and Mobility, 21*, 13–25.

Hesse-Biber, S. N. & Leavy, P. (2006). *The practice of qualitative research*. London: Sage.

Hislop, D. (2005). *Knowledge management in organizations. A critical introduction*. Oxford: Oxford University Press.

Hollis, M. (1994). *The philosophy of social science*. Cambridge: Cambridge university press.

Hunter, J. E. & Schmidt, F. L. (1990). *Methods of meta-analysis: correcting error and bias in research findings*. Newbury Park, CA: Sage.

Hussey, J. & Hussey, R. (1997). *Business research: a practical guide for undergraduate and postgraduate students*. London: MacMillan.

ISCU Report (2004). *Optimizing knowledge in the information society*.

Jashapara, A. (2004). *Knowledge management*. Harlow: Pearson Education.

Kerlinger, F. N. (1973). *Foundations of behavioral research*. Tokyo: Holt-Saunders Japan.

Kottak, C. P. (2004). *Anthropology; the exploration of human diversity*. New York: Mc Graw Hill.

Leiber, J. (2001). *A philosophical glossary*. Houston, TX: University of Houston.

Marshall, C. & Rossman, G. B. (1999). *Designing qualitative research*. London: Sage.

Miles, M. B. & Huberman, A. M. (1994). *Qualitative data analysis*. Thousand Oaks, CA: Sage.

Patching, D. (1999). *Practical soft systems analysis*. London: Pitman publishing.

Pidgeon, N. F., Turner, B. A., & Blockley, D. I. (1991). The use of grounded theory for conceptual analysis in knowledge elicitation. *International Journal of Man-Machine Studies, 35*(2), 151–173.

Ragin, C. (1994). *Constructing social research*. Thousand Oaks, CA: Sage.

Reason, P. (1999). *Integrating action and reflection through co-operative inquiry*. London: Sage.

Robson, C. (2002). *Real word research*. Oxford: Blackwell.

Salkind, N. J. (2000). *Exploring research*. New Jersey: Prentice Hall.

Sartori, G. (1984). *Social Science concepts*. London: Sage.

Schatzman, L. & Strauss, A. L. (1973). *Field research*. New Jersey: Prentice Hall.

Stake, R. E. (1995). *The art of case study research*. London: Sage.

Strauss, A. L. (1987). *Qualitative analysis for social scientists*. Cambridge: Cambridge University Press.

Straus, C. & Corbin, J. (1998). *Basics of qualitative research: techniques and procedures for developing grounded theory*. London: Sage.

The American Heritage Dictionary of the English Language (4th ed.) (2000). Boston, MA: Houghton Mifflin Company.

Thomas, A. B. (2004). *Research skills for management studies*. London: Routledge.

Vygotskii, L. S. (1993). *Collected works of L.S. Vygotskii*. Deventer: Kluwer.

Websters' Comprehensive Dictionary (1996). Chicago: Ferguson Publishing Company.

Yin, R. K. (2003). *Case study research: design and methods*. London: Sage.

Websites

Dick, B. (1999). What is action research? http://www.scu.edu.au/schools/gcm/ar/arhome.html.

Encarta World English Dictionary (2004). http://encarta.msn.com/encnet/features/dictionary/dictionaryhome.aspx

Kemerling, G. (2002). Philosophy pages. http://www.philosophypages.com/

Levi-Faur, D. (2003). Comparative methods dictionary. http://poli.haifa.ac.il/~levi/dictionary.html

WordNet 2.0, Princeton University (2003). http://wordnet.princeton.edu/

Writing@CSU (1993–2006). http://writing.colostate.edu/guides/research/glossary/

Lightning Source UK Ltd.
Milton Keynes UK
14 March 2010

151311UK00008BB/55/P